PRAISE FOR *REIGNITING THE HUMAN CONNECTION*

"*Reigniting the Human Connection: A Pathway to Diversity, Inclusion, and Health Equity* is a reminder of the importance of the human touch in medicine and healthcare. This book provides a holistic framework for embedding the tenets of health equity into the healthcare delivery system."

—CHERYL PEGUS, MD, MPH
Managing Director, Morgan Health Ventures
Director, Alice L. Walton School of Medicine
Former Executive Vice President, Health and Wellness, Walmart

"Mieres, McCulloch, and Wright's dedication to advancing the cause of greater diversity, inclusion, and equity to ensure high-quality health outcomes for patients and communities served by Northwell Health is inspiring. The pathway described in their practical, powerful book draws from their remarkable experience in offering a meaningful, humane approach for navigating our rapidly evolving healthcare system. For the sake of all our children and all the children to come, each and every one of us must lead, in whatever way we can, and strive to bring others along with us to a better, fairer, more peaceful tomorrow. I am grateful to have had the opportunity to learn from these outstanding members of the caring Northwell Health community how to accelerate that movement."

—STEWART FRIEDMAN, PhD
Emeritus Professor of Management Practice, The Wharton School
CEO, Total Leadership
Author: Parents Who Lead: The Leadership Approach You Need To Parent with Purpose, Fuel Your Career, and Create a Richer Life

"*Reigniting The Human Connection: A Pathway to Diversity, Inclusion, and Health Equity* is a must-read for those in healthcare and beyond. Healthcare is in urgent need of redesign to eliminate barriers, address inequities, and influence positive change needed to improve health outcomes for all. Dr. Mieres and coauthors not only brilliantly lay out the problem, but most importantly, they provide solutions!"

—DON LEMON

Former Anchor, CNN Tonight
Author, This Is the Fire: What I Say to My Friends About Racism

"My colleagues at Northwell Health, under the leadership of an extraordinarily passionate leader, Michael Dowling, have provided us with an innovative and disruptive forensic dissection of the elements necessary to achieve health equity in any community, nation, or the world. This is a very timely and much-needed work based on their decades of study and multidisciplinary commitment to ensuring that all persons have the opportunity to achieve optimal health. This book should be required reading for all health professionals and elected leadership who are entrusted with generating health-related policy that benefits those citizens that they have the privilege to serve."

—RICHARD CARMONA, MD, MPH, FACS

17th Surgeon General of the United States
Distinguished Professor, University of Arizona

"DiversityInc has measured effective diversity, inclusion, and equity strategies across all industries in the US for over twenty years. Northwell Health, New York State's largest healthcare provider and private employer, has made the list for the ninth straight year and remained in the top spot in the 2021 DiversityInc rankings for hospitals and health systems.

Northwell is also recognized in four other DiversityInc specialty lists. These ranks are a reflection of Northwell Health's decade-long journey toward the tenets of diversity, inclusion, and health equity for its team members, patients, and communities. Further, and in partnership with the Healthcare Anchor Network, Northwell is one of the first health systems to declare racism as a public health crisis. This leadership accountability, exemplified at Northwell Health by CEO Michael Dowling, is foundational to achieving and maintaining health equity. DiversityInc celebrates with Northwell Health as Drs. Mieres, McCulloch, and Wright publish *Reigniting the Human Connection: A Pathway to Diversity, Inclusion, and Health Equity* to provide best-in-class strategies to ensure sustainable equity, diversity, and inclusion outcomes for diverse workforces, patients, and communities."

—CAROLYNN JOHNSON
Former CEO, Fair360, Formerly DiversityInc

"*Reigniting the Human Connection* amplifies the major lessons from COVID-19 in addressing health equity with communities of color disproportionately impacted. It is an urgent call to action for the US healthcare system."

—ROHINI ANAND, PhD
CEO, Rohini Anand LLC
Former Global SVP, Corporate Responsibility and Global Chief Diversity Officer, Sodexo
Author, Leading Global Diversity, Equity, and Inclusion: A Guide for Systemic Change in Multinational Organizations

"We're approaching an inflection point in healthcare, and we can no longer afford to embrace a partial commitment to accessibility, quality, and equity in an increasingly complex and ever-changing healthcare environment. This book not only lays the groundwork for a transformation in how we think about advancing health equity but will also serve as an essential and practical tool for healthcare change agents. *Reigniting the Human Connection: The Pathway to Diversity, Inclusion, and Health Equity* is the most important book written on the biggest challenge confronting healthcare leaders and providers."

—DANIEL E. DAWES, JD
Executive Director, Satcher Health Leadership Institute, Morehouse School of Medicine
Author, The Political Determinants of Health
Founding Dean, School of Global Health, Meharry Medical College

"This book captures the critically important work of advancing diversity, equity, and inclusion in healthcare and lays a foundation for other health systems and caregivers who follow this path. As a cardiologist focused on sex- and gender-based cardiology and who has led efforts to advance diversity, equity, and inclusion, I know that those health systems that embrace these changes will benefit the communities they serve, their people, and their patients. Congratulations to Dr. Mieres and colleagues on leading the way for so many others."

—PAMELA S. DOUGLAS, MD, MACC
Ursula Geller Professor of Research in Cardiovascular Diseases, Department of Medicine, Duke University
Director of the Multimodality Imaging Program, Duke Clinical Research Institute

"In *Reigniting the Human Connection*, the authors, whom I have had the pleasure of knowing and working with over the years, provide a thoughtful, timely, and much-needed assessment of healthcare, centering diversity, equity, and inclusion in ways that demonstrate this work is a *need to do*, not a *nice to do*, in today's world. Comprehensive, evidence-based, and built on real-world experience, this is a must-read for those in this work now and interested in this work in the future."

—JOSEPH R. BETANCOURT, MD, MPH
Associate Professor Of Medicine, Harvard Medical School
Former Senior Vice President, Equity and Community Health
Founder, The Disparities Solutions Center, Massachusetts General Hospital
President, The Commonwealth Fund

"At the beginning of this important and insightful book, the authors explain their bold mission to ask difficult questions about health disparities and the way we approach healthcare in this country. Readers will be inspired by their honest approach in seeking answers and also by their insistence that the way forward will involve efforts to recast healthcare as a partnership involving providers and patients."

—FREEMAN HRABROWSKI, PhD

Former President, University of Maryland, Baltimore County
Author, The Empowered University: Shared Leadership, Culture Change, and Academic Success

"What does real diversity look like, and why is it worth working toward? How do we build and sustain systems that work for all of us? In this timely work, leaders from New York's largest health system detail their decade-long quest to advance diversity, equity, and inclusion in healthcare. Healthcare is the profession that first sees how diversity evolves. Drawing from real-world patient experiences and their own lessons learned, they offer practical strategies for building systems grounded in empathy, community partnership, holistic approaches to patients and care, and the recognition of our shared humanity. Optimistic and wide-ranging and reflective of the need for new strategies, *Reigniting the Human Connection* presents a vision of what a more equitable healthcare system could be and a roadmap for how to get there."

—STEVE PEMBERTON

Chief People Officer, Franworth
Former Chief Human Resources Officer, Workhuman
Best-Selling Author, The Lighthouse Effect *and* A Chance in the World

"I applaud the authors of this book as they provide the health-care industry a best-practice framework based upon a decade of applied experience using the tenets of diversity, inclusion, and health equity within one of the most diverse cities in the world to improve the health outcomes of the patients and communities served. Your leadership in taking on this serious issue and making it a part of your lived mission is exemplary and deserves to be celebrated."

—HOWARD J. ROSS
Social Justice Advocate
Author, ReInventing Diversity: Transforming Organizational Community to Strengthen People, Purpose and Performance*;* Everyday Bias: Identifying and Navigating Unconscious Judgments in Our Daily Lives *and* Our Search for Belonging: How Our Need to Connect Is Tearing Us Apart

"To address our unmet global health disparities, it is imperative that we utilize an equity lens that prioritizes the needs of socio-economically and racially/ethnically disadvantaged persons. *Reigniting the Human Connection: A Pathway to Diversity, Inclusion, and Health Equity* offers solutions to embed the equity lens into healthcare delivery."

—MICHELLE A. ALBERT, MD, MPH, FACC, FAHA
Walter A. Haas-Lucie Stern Endowed Chair in Cardiology
Professor of Medicine and Director, Center for the Study of Adversity and Cardiovascular Disease (NURTURE Center)
Associate Dean of Admissions, UCSF School of Medicine
Former President, American Heart Association
Former President, Association of Black Cardiologists, Inc.Former
Former President, Association of University Cardiologists

"Why is yet another treatise addressing diversity, equity, and inclusion necessary? This expository work describing a success model fuels those of us seeking equity, especially health equity. Led by established national leaders in diversity, equity, and inclusion, Mieres and colleagues delve into a ten-year journey sourced within a model institution built upon an ethos of change. Too often the justification for important discussions addressing DEI are couched around business imperatives: improving economic productivity; expanding the market; responding to external insistences; and checking the boxes. What's missing in so many discussions and subsequent initiatives is the human connection. Perhaps that's why success is either fleeting or nonexistent. This book appeals to our 'better angels'; the book reminds us not only of the social determinants of health but also the moral determinants of health. We are reminded that, when we change our lens, what we see changes and we are called to rapt attention by the keen awareness that our society, any society, is defined by how we treat those who are most vulnerable. It is our 'better angels' who reset the moral compass and ignite more purposeful and more just DEI efforts. We do this not with vapid metrics or hollow strategic plans but by revisiting and then reigniting the human connection. It is our humanness that we crave. Without the human connection, what do we become? Read, study, and actualize the work of these brilliant social architects: Mieres, McCulloch, and Wright."

—CLYDE W. YANCY, MD, MSC

Chief of Cardiology, Department of Medicine
Vice Dean for Diversity and Inclusion
Professor of Medicine (Cardiology) and Medical Social Sciences,
Feinberg School of Medicine at Northwestern University

"The dual pandemics of our time, one biologic and one cultural, and academic medicine's response to them are the subject of the remarkable treatise of *Reigniting the Human Connection: A Pathway to Diversity, Inclusion and Health Equity*. That human connection is the reality of humanism in healthcare, which we define as compassionate, collaborative, and scientifically excellent care, a gold standard that quiets old understandings in favor of the twenty-first-century possibility of transformation and cure for both COVID-19 and racism. The book, by Dr. Jennifer Mieres and colleagues at Northwell Health, is both an explication of why the wondrous age of medical technology requires an equal focus on humanism and a manual for achieving this transformation in academic health centers. The authors show the way to create this future by sharing a framework for systems and cultures that support humanistic care for all. This lucid work makes an intelligible case for care that sees all patients as humans, not diseases and illuminates the path ahead in high resolution. Its audience is the entire membership of the healthcare team and its administrators"

—RICHARD I. LEVIN, MD
Immediate Past President and Former CEO, Arnold P. Gold Foundation

PRAISE FROM THE TEAM AT NORTHWELL HEALTH

"At Northwell Health, we are committed to our mission to raise the health of our communities. We are New York's largest healthcare provider—and we take that responsibility seriously. We know that caring for people clinically is not enough, so we think creatively to solve for the social, economic, and environmental circumstances of our patients. The COVID-19 pandemic demonstrated our ability as healthcare leaders to problem solve and to innovate. Based upon this, our call to action, as Drs. Mieres, McCulloch, and Wright highlight in their book, *Reigniting the Human Connection: A Pathway to Diversity, Inclusion, and Health Equity*, is to build upon this spirit of innovation to continue fostering trusted partnerships with the diverse communities we live in and serve."

—MARK SOLAZZO
President, Strategic Initiatives, and COO, Northwell Health

"*Reigniting the Human Connection: A Pathway to Diversity, Inclusion, and Health Equity* is a must-read for insight on the journey of an organization (and its leaders) in developing best practices in diversity, inclusion, and health equity, the lessons learned over the last ten years, and how the COVID-19 crisis accelerated these efforts."

—DEBBIE SALAS-LOPEZ, MD, MPH
Senior Vice President, Department of Community and Population Health, Northwell Health

"This book deals with essential elements of effective healthcare that must be understood and incorporated into both the strategic and daily efforts of our workforce. We must create a diverse workforce that uses equity and inclusivity as major metrics of success. It must start during the education and training of that workforce.

Eradicating health disparities can only happen when caregivers and policymakers understand the impact of the social determinants of health, the need for the workforce to come from all of the groups that are our patients, and that this will only happen by intentional efforts, programs, and metrics that will push us to settle for nothing less than true health equity and inclusion. It starts with educating a diverse workforce and ends with our patients feeling safe, trusted, confident, respected, and cared for equitably and expertly.

The role of our school is so much a part of this, beginning with our Pipeline Programs, then our curriculum, our culture, and finally the values we try to instill in all of our graduates. This book tells a story of Northwell Health and its efforts at equity and inclusivity and the home it has made for our school of medicine."

—LAWRENCE G. SMITH, MD, MACP
Dean Emeritus, Donald and Barbara Zucker School of Medicine at Hofstra/Northwell
Former Executive Vice President and Physician-in-Chief

"There's nothing like sitting down with somebody to ask them about themselves and really caring about them. I think when you make that human connection, it's so powerful, whether it's an employee, physician, or patient. With this human connection, we gain a greater understanding of an individual's life journey and how we might be able to assist them in achieving their wishes moving forward. This is the greatest legacy any of us can leave—assisting others in achieving their dreams, aspirations, and wishes in life."

—MAUREEN T. WHITE, RN, MBA, NEA-BC, FNAP, FAAN
Executive Vice President and Chief Nurse Executive, Margaret Crotty and Rory Riggs Clinical Chair in Nursing, Northwell Health

"The path forward requires our commitment to transforming the conditions of historically marginalized communities; improving the quality of housing and neighborhood environments of these populations; advocating for policies that eliminate inequities in access to economic opportunities, quality education, and healthcare; and enhancing allyship among racial and ethnic groups. *Reigniting the Human Connection: A Pathway to Diversity, Inclusion, and Health Equity* represents a tried-and-true framework to help healthcare organizations in putting the patient as partner, where we can move from being a healthcare institution for the sick to one of wellness and prevention."

—DAVID L. BATTINELLI, MD
Executive Vice President and Physician-in-Chief
Dean and Betsey Cushing Whitney Professor of Medicine, Donald and Barbara Zucker School of Medicine at Hofstra/Northwell

"Achieving equity, diversity, inclusion, and belonging is key to delivering on our mission, performance outcomes, and commitment to remaining a great place to work ... for all. It defines our character and identity as an organization, and in its absence, we cannot truly claim victory in serving our diverse communities and attracting and retaining a diverse and talented workforce."

—MAXINE CARRINGTON, JD
Senior Vice President and Chief People Officer

"When Amanda Gorman, a twenty-two-year-old poet, shared the words of her poem 'The Hill We Climb' at the inauguration of President Biden, she spoke that America is a 'nation that isn't broken but simply unfinished.' This book attempts to tackle one of the major unfinished challenges that America's healthcare system must confront in the years ahead: achieving health equity for all of its citizens. The authors of this book recognize that a foundational element of achieving health equity is to develop and support a culture that embraces humanism in healthcare. They identify a framework on how to think about this challenge and provide a number of concrete steps that leaders and organizations can take that ultimately will move our nation closer to the promise of providing equitable care for all. This is an invaluable resource for all health providers trying to address America's unfinished business."

—JEFFREY KRAUT
Executive Vice President, Strategy and Analytics, Chair, NYS
Public Health and Health Planning Council
Associate Dean, Strategy, Donald and Barbara Zucker School of
Medicine at Hofstra/Northwell

REIGNITING THE HUMAN CONNECTION

REIGNITING THE HUMAN CONNECTION

A **PATHWAY TO** DIVERSITY, INCLUSION, AND **HEALTH EQUITY**

JENNIFER H. MIERES, MD

ELIZABETH C. McCULLOCH, PhD

MICHAEL P. WRIGHT, EdD

ForbesBooks

Published by ForbesBooks, Charleston, South Carolina.
Member of Advantage Media Group.

ForbesBooks is a registered trademark, and the ForbesBooks colophon is a trademark of Forbes Media, LLC.

Printed in the United States of America.

10 9 8 7 6 5 4 3 2 1

ISBN: 978-1-955884-11-2 (Hardcover)
ISBN: 979-8-88750-522-0 (Paperback)
LCCN: 2021924972

Cover design by Carly Blake.
Layout design by Mary Hamilton.

Advantage Media Group is proud to be a part of the Tree Neutral® program. Tree Neutral offsets the number of trees consumed in the production and printing of this book by taking proactive steps such as planting trees in direct proportion to the number of trees used to print books. To learn more about Tree Neutral, please visit www.treeneutral.com.

Since 1917, Forbes has remained steadfast in its mission to serve as the defining voice of entrepreneurial capitalism. ForbesBooks, launched in 2016 through a partnership with Advantage Media Group, furthers that aim by helping business and thought leaders bring their stories, passion, and knowledge to the forefront in custom books. Opinions expressed by ForbesBooks authors are their own. To be considered for publication, please visit www.forbesbooks.com.

In memory of our beloved colleague and friend Marilyn Dienstag. A nurse and integral team member of the Northwell Health Center for Equity of Care, Marilyn embodied the characteristics we see as foundational in humanistic care. We view this book as part of her legacy, one that illustrates many aspects of both the need for and the benefit of nurturing human connections in healthcare.

CONTENTS

PART I

A MAP FOR ACCOMPLISHING NEEDED CHANGE

A FRAMEWORK FOR DIVERSITY, INCLUSION, AND HEALTH EQUITY

CREATING A FRAMEWORK FOR SUSTAINABLE CHANGE

PART II

BUILDING A FRAMEWORK FOR DIVERSITY, INCLUSION, AND HEALTH EQUITY

LEADERSHIP COMMITMENT

EDUCATION AND DEVELOPMENT

LANGUAGE ACCESS

COMMUNITY PARTNERSHIP

SUPPLIER DIVERSITY

FOREWORD

BY MICHAEL J. DOWLING

We are at a landmark moment and critical juncture in US health-care. The health disparities unmasked by COVID-19 made it abundantly clear that when we do not take care of everyone in our society, all of society suffers. It is a hard-earned lesson that must forever reshape our traditional healthcare delivery model and catapult a much-needed redesign aimed at ensuring equitable care for all. As demonstrated by the dedication shown by our healthcare professionals during the pandemic, human connections will be instrumental in rebuilding trust within communities that bore the brunt of the pain and suffering.

Despite the recent heroics of our nation's caregivers, there are many distractions and influences in the day-to-day practice of medicine that inhibit their ability to give patients the time and attention needed to truly understand the issues affecting their health and well-being. Certainly, these are not deliberate oversights by clinicians but the result of time constraints, rising caseloads, a growing reliance on technology, the increasing requirements for documentation, a lack of cultural awareness, and numerous other factors that are eroding the human connection between caregivers and patients.

As its authors so eloquently articulate, this book is a call to action to advance human connections in healthcare. It is a simple but radical solution to narrowing the huge gaps in life expectancy between rich and poor and to healing a nation where 80 percent of health problems are caused by lifestyle factors.

The authors offer insight from the lessons learned from Northwell Health's decade-long, formalized strategy toward greater equity in healthcare and greater diversity across all levels of the health system. They provide concrete examples of how we can ensure that human connection remains an integral element of healthcare delivery and how principles of diversity and efforts to improve health equity and outcomes can be infused into the tapestry of the twenty-first-century healthcare model. As such, this book provides healthcare leaders and change agents an opportunity to define their own roadmap for embedding the tenets of diversity, inclusion, and health equity for their team members, patients, and communities served. The book may also validate and inform your existing approach toward equitable healthcare delivery.

While the COVID-19 pandemic unmasked the disparities that still exist in our communities, we have proven through our community partnerships that we can effectively respond to these events. Healthcare delivery may be in a constant state of flux, but at its core, it is a human enterprise—people caring for people.

In confronting crises like COVID-19 and chronic illnesses that disproportionately impact vulnerable communities, specifically those of color and or lower socioeconomic status, we all need to embrace an expanded approach to healthcare delivery that considers culture, spiritual beliefs, health access, and literacy.

The more we think about how race, gender, ethnicity, sexual orientation, age, mental health, disability, geographic location, and other factors dictate the health and wellness of those we serve, the better we can serve them. Humanism in healthcare calls on us to be productive change agents at work and in our society.

We as healthcare providers must continually remind ourselves why we entered this profession—to care for individuals in need, regardless of race, religion, or financial status. Humanism invites patients into the healing process, helping them to truly understand their illness and partner to find the right path that fits their needs.

We have come a long way in recognizing and acknowledging health disparities and scrutinizing the ways we can continue to change those paradigms. This is our perpetual call to action. Though it may never be fully completed, we have no doubt that what we ultimately build will be strong and make a difference in people's day-to-day lives. But it takes a strong and unified voice. In short, it takes leadership. I call on my fellow healthcare leaders nationwide to join me in Reigniting the Human Connection.

—MICHAEL J. DOWLING
President and CEO, Northwell Health
Coauthor, After the Roof Caved In: An Immigrant's Journey from Ireland to America, Leading Through a Pandemic, *and* Health Care Reboot: Megatrends Energizing American Medicine

ACKNOWLEDGMENTS

When you change the way you look at things,
the things you look at change.

—DR. WAYNE DYER

First and foremost, we would like to thank Mark Leichliter for his endless insight, instrumental guidance, and invaluable constructive critique. We value you as a professional but count you as a friend. Also, a very special thank-you to our partners at Forbes for their thoughtful support as we embarked on this journey.

Over the last ten years, we have evolved our healthcare delivery model to incorporate the tenets of diversity, inclusion, and health equity to meet the healthcare needs of our diverse communities.

This journey to achieve health equity has been akin to climbing Mount Everest, and we have made it to the first summit. Our climb would not be possible without the incredible commitment, leadership support, and guidance from our fearless commander in chief, Michael

J. Dowling, and our chief operating officer, Mark Solazzo. Heartfelt acknowledgment to the board of trustees of Northwell Health and our Committee on Community Health for their dedication and leadership commitment to ensuring the health and well-being of our communities.

We also want to express our deep gratitude to our amazing partners at Northwell Health who have been steadfast champions of this important work within our organization and communities served, including Kathleen Gallo, RN, PhD; Dr. Lawrence Smith; Maureen White, RN; Eugene Tangney; Joseph Moscola, PA; Maxine Carrington, JD; Dr. David Battinelli; Ramon Soto; Dr. Stacey Rosen; Ralph Nappi; and Terry Lynam.

Additionally, we are honored to acknowledge the dedicated commitment of our strategic partners who have been coarchitects with us in designing and sustaining the tenets of diversity, inclusion, and health equity for our team members, patients, and communities. Without you, this journey would not have been successful. Special shout-outs to Jeffrey Kraut; Michele Cusack; Kevin Beiner; Stephen Bello; Dr. Jason Naidich; Dr. Ira Nash; Dr. Mark Jarrett; Dr. Andrew Yacht; Dr. Debbie Salas-Lopez; Dr. Robert Roswell; Dr. Charles Schleien; Dr. Zenobia Brown; Michael Goldberg; Jon Sendach; Dr. Thomas McGinn; Deborah Schiff; Joseph Schulman; Merryl Siegel; Karina Davidson, PhD; David Gill; Thomas Sclafani; Dr. Christina Brennan; Reverend Barbara Felker; Edward Fraser; Rebecca Gordon; Sven Gierlinger; Agnes Barden, DNP; Donna Drummond; Phyllis McCready; Yosef Dlugacz, PhD; Dr. Annabella Salvador; Dr. Mark Schiffer; Dr. David Langer; Launette Woolforde, EdD, DNP; Brian Lally; John Bosco; Dr. David W. Rosenthal; Laurence Kraemer, JD; Rita Mercieca, RN; Richard Miller; Zachary Klein; Jeanne Gabriel; Jacquelyn Pupelis; Geraldine Sikes; Dr. Sharonne Hayes; Dr. Kimberlydawn Wisdom; Jack Tocco; Laura Carlo; Patricia McMenanim; Mark

Tursi; Dr. Ernesto Molmenti; Mark Gloade, JD; Alexandra Trinkoff, JD; Dr. David Hirschwerk; Karen Nelson, RN; Barbara Osborn; Patti Adelman, EdD; Jonathan Plissner, JD; Andrea DeLoney; Alice Fornari, EdD; Catherine Bangeranye, PhD; Marcella De Geronimo; Dawn Wells; Dr. Jill Kalman; Dr. Dan Baker; Michelle Freel; Alex Hellinger, DPT; Dr. Varinder Singh; Dr. Jeffrey Kuvin; our friends at Katz Institute for Women's Health; and all of our Business Employee Resource Group leaders and executive sponsors.

Idowu Koyenikan wrote, "There is immense power when a group of people with similar interests get together to work on the same goals." We could not have accomplished this journey without the passion, dedication, and selfless commitment of our Center for Equity of Care family, including Dr. Johanna Martinez; Dr. Penny Stern; Anu Anish; Richard LaRochelle; Samantha Rosario; Neela Gomes; Colleen Ruggerio; Lori Loose; Cynthia Lewin; Beatrice Walsh; Dr. Elizabeth Maltin; Natanique Williams; Rosagna Mancebo; and Lori Russo. Our collective journey has inspired and fueled why we got into healthcare in the first place—to improve the health outcomes of all we serve. We are honored to be friends on this journey and truly grateful for this team for living into what it means to reignite the human connection in healthcare.

We also want to thank our frontline team members, who put their lives on the line during the peak of the COVID-19 pandemic. You are true heroes. We honor you for your service and dedication to the health and well-being of our communities.

Lastly, we would like to thank our families and friends for being our tireless champions and inspiration during this incredible journey.

*People heal from their pain when they have
authentic human connection.*

—MARSHALL B. ROSENBERG

A JOURNEY TOWARD HEALTH EQUITY

Ring the bells that still can ring
Forget your perfect offering
There is a crack, a crack in everything
That's how the light gets in.

—FROM "ANTHEM," BY LEONARD COHEN

During the worst surge of the 2020 COVID-19 pandemic, no health organization in the United States cared for more COVID-19 patients than Northwell Health, where we are privileged to work. Headquartered in New Hyde Park, New York, with roots firmly planted on Long Island, and now with twenty-three hospitals and nearly 830 outpatient facilities spanning New York City, Long Island, and Westchester County, Northwell Health caregivers were at the epicenter of COVID-19's grip. About the time we emerged from the spring 2020 first wave of the crisis and began to assess the full scope of its impact, the leadership team of our health system displayed a beautiful, striking image at its corporate headquarters. The image featured, from a patient's view, three masked and gowned caregivers leaning in, their eyes filled with compassion and healing. The image was a mosaic, one artfully and intricately constructed from thousands of photographs of our team members and interspersed with a repeated tiny, hand-drawn depiction of a heart. The image not only celebrates the humanist compassion and dedication of our staff, but its construction—a mosaic of faces—also echoes the immense diversity of the communities, team members, and patients we serve and of the people who make up our system.

Installed in May 2020 at Northwell's corporate headquarters in New Hyde Park, NY, this beautiful, 18' x 25' mosaic was designed using images of Northwell team members and their supporters, representing the health system's thousands of #HealthcareHeroes fighting on the frontlines of the COVID-19 pandemic. Source: Northwell Health

The Northwell Health service area (see map on next page) reaches at least eight million New Yorkers, providing healthcare to one of the most diverse patient populations in the United States. We treat more than two million patients annually. If you were an artist seeking inspiration for a mosaic representing the diverse array of faces that reflect the American multicultural experiment, the halls of Northwell Health's hospitals, ambulatory practices, academic centers, and research facilities would prove an ideal place to visit. In Queens alone, 176 languages are spoken. Half the health system's patients speak English as a second language or don't speak it at all. A patient entering one of our facilities might be a newly arrived immigrant with virtually no local familial ties or a fourth-generation business owner who can give you a detailed history of every business on their block. Our patients are as likely to be a Wall Street broker as an Uber driver, a hair stylist, or a fast-food worker. We serve neighborhoods where the dominant language might be Spanish, or it might be Polish, and if Spanish, you might hear dialects from several dozen countries of origin. Step out our doors, and you're likely to be within easy walking distance of synagogues, mosques, temples, prayer centers, fellowships, cathedrals, and Christian churches, representing as many different denominations as you could name. Along your walk, you would encounter every chain store and restaurant you might find replicated virtually anywhere in the country as well as shops, grocery stores, boutiques, cafés, and salons, as specialized to the needs and tastes of myriad cultures, diets, and preferences as there are variations of skin tone across the human species.

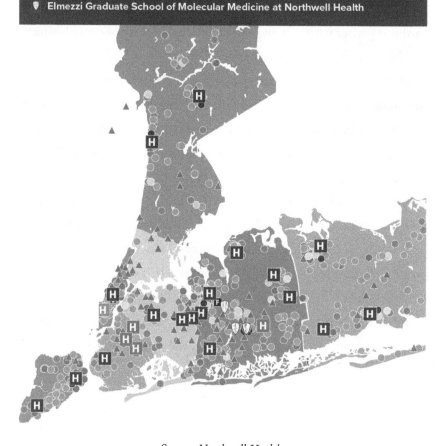

Legend:

- H Hospitals
- F Feinstein Institutes
- H Lenox Health Greenwich Village
- ✳ Manhattan Eye, Ear, & Throat Hospital
- H Safety Net Partners
- ● Ambulatory Surgery Centers
- ○ Cancer Centers
- △ Community Partnerships
- ● Dialysis Centers
- ● Imaging Centers
- ● Lab Patient Service Centers
- ● Primary Care Locations
- ● Specialty Care Locations
- ● Urgent Care Centers
- ⚕ Donald and Barbara Zucker School of Medicine at Hofstra / Northwell
- ⚕ Hofstra Northwell School of Graduate Nursing and Physician Assistant Studies
- ⚕ Elmezzi Graduate School of Molecular Medicine at Northwell Health

Source: Northwell Health

Yet every patient who enters our doors is as unique as the genetic cells of which they are made. Their stories are as diverse as their biology. We believe the COVID-19 crisis that gave rise to the mosaic offers a pivotal moment in public awareness and discourse to address the experiences of these diverse individuals, for it has exposed the disparity of healthcare present in our nation with a clarity most have never encountered before. While we see COVID-19 as a catalyst for amplifying discussion on the issues of inequitable care, the disparities it has highlighted are nothing new. Indeed, we align with a number of our colleagues around the country in the belief that what we have faced with COVID-19 is not a pandemic but a syndemic.[1] The notion of a syndemic was first conceived by Merrill Singer, an American medical anthropologist. In recent applications, the use of the word *syndemic* has expanded beyond Singer's original definition regarding diseases interacting within the human body and now is used to reference a "conceptual framework for understanding diseases or health conditions that arise in populations and that are exacerbated by the social, economic, environmental, and political milieu in which a population is immersed."[2]

We support this use of the term syndemic because it incorporates a vital truth about a holistic vision of health:

> *The vulnerability of older citizens; Black, Asian, and minority ethnic communities; and key workers who are commonly poorly paid with fewer welfare protections points to a truth so far barely acknowledged—namely, that no matter how effective a treatment or protective a vaccine, the pursuit of a purely biomedical solution to COVID-19 will fail.*[3]

The vulnerability of believing that health is impacted only when patients are present while inside clinical settings was well known long before the world ever heard of COVID-19. We have spent the last ten years building a system-wide framework for addressing such vulnerability, and we've done so from an awareness that to resolve healthcare disparities, we must act on a holistic vision of health. Seeing the mosaic image we referenced at the outset of this introduction—or, indeed, any number of images of the healthcare professionals who tended to those flooding ICUs around the world throughout the COVID-19 pandemic—we recognize that there are plenty of caring people who value the human connections required to care for sick patients. There will never be a shortage of those willing to tend to a bedside or to squeeze an ailing patient's hand. So why are we calling for "reigniting the human connection in healthcare"? Because while masks became a reality for the need to protect against a dangerous, highly contagious virus, we've too long donned other kinds of symbolic masks that create distance from patients: an ever-increasing dependence on technology, greater specialization and the resultant fragmentation of patient experiences, corporatization of the practice of medicine, the shift in priority for business and finance in medicine, reduced time in patient encounters, and a deemphasis on the humanities in the education of physicians. Many of these factors were important underpinnings to why Dr. Arnold Gold, and now the foundation named after him, recognized that we had created a healthcare environment where physician trainees were scientifically proficient and technically well-trained but often demonstrated a sad lack of caring and compassion.

Moreover, there is a through line between these sorts of dehumanizing elements of modern healthcare and the forces that create inequities in patient treatment. The common denominator for both is a lack of empathy. When healthcare providers cannot understand the perspectives and experiences of their patients, this lack of empathy can impact the way they treat patients *and* how patients regard healthcare providers, institutions, and even policy. Empathy resides at the heart of human connections. When empathetic connections are severed, health disparities result. Such health disparities have a long history, as starkly revealed when W. E. B. Du Bois wrote in his 1899 book *The Philadelphia Negro*: "The most difficult social problem in the matter of Negro health is the peculiar attitude of the nation toward the well-being of the race. There have [...] been few other cases in the history of civilized peoples where human suffering has been viewed with such peculiar indifference."[4] Indifference breeds distrust. With well-documented, widely known examples of inhumane treatment of Black patients—from the gruesome experiments on enslaved people to the forced sterilizations of Black women or the infamous Tuskegee syphilis study that withheld treatment from hundreds of Black men for decades—distrust seems a perfectly logical response within Black communities. Should we be surprised then that more Blacks were slower to receive vaccinations against COVID-19 than other racial groups?[5] The needed revolution of reigniting the human connection in healthcare starts by understanding patients, their perspectives, and their personal and cultural histories. Those are all actions of empathy.

As we will detail in the book, patient behavior has changed significantly, as has patient access to healthcare information (note here that while access to healthcare information is omnipresent, access to *accurate* healthcare information or improved health literacy is not). To a large extent, healthcare professionals' training and behaviors, including the practice of empathy, have not kept the same pace of change. What has been lost along the way is a better understanding of their patients, particularly as patient demographics also change rapidly. As a result, the gulf between patients and the healthcare professionals' experiences has grown. Shrinking that gulf starts by reforming human connections between patients and those healthcare professionals who serve them. Doing so is a foundational step on the journey toward achieving greater diversity in healthcare settings. In turn, a more diverse healthcare workforce and one that can reach across divides is required to develop the education necessary to realizing inclusion. Both diversity and inclusion must become systemically present throughout healthcare systems if we are ever to realize health equity.

What COVID-19 has revealed makes for an important inflection point to drive change, but the interests of this book go far beyond this specific syndemic. We will occasionally draw examples from the COVID-19 era because of the importance of its tipping point and because much of this text was written while the world was in its grip, but we also range far and wide, within our own health system and without, for other illustrations of both the problems of health inequities and the vehicles for their solution. Nothing less than a national reignition for the value of the human connection throughout healthcare, one that acknowledges the interconnectivity between biology, disease, and the social determinants of health, will solve healthcare inequity.

In order to treat the whole human, we must first see patients as people. Consider just a few microcosmic snapshots, some famous in medical chronicles and others personal to Northwell Health that can reveal the risk of not recognizing the individual needs of the patients we treat as we form a different sort of healthcare mosaic:

- Eighteen-year-old Cuban American WR was out with a friend when he experienced a headache, which he attributed either to the smell of gasoline in his friend's car or a fast-food meal he had consumed. He ignored his discomfort and his symptoms for several hours. Later that evening, after collapsing outside his girlfriend's house, he was taken to a South Florida hospital by ambulance and arrived in a comatose state. Emergency room and ICU personnel erroneously believed that WR had suffered an intentional drug overdose and treated him accordingly. They had reached this conclusion without a neurological consult based on the initial physical exam, a severely incomplete medical history, and in large part, a bad misunderstanding. Family members and friends accompanying WR in the ER used the same word he had applied to his condition: *intoxicado*. Among Cubans, "intoxicado" is an all-encompassing word that means there's something wrong, often because of consuming bad food. The medical staff keyed on the word and, without knowledge of its Cuban associations and taking a "Spanglish" stab, assumed it meant "intoxicated." The miscommunication was amplified by what the family admitted was habitual deference to doctors and reluctance to challenge their diagnoses. WR had actually suffered an intracerebellar hemorrhage that continued to bleed for more than two days as he lay unconscious in the hospital. He was left a quadriplegic.

- JL, a fifty-two-year-old White male, reluctantly agreed, at his wife's insistence, to a stress test after experiencing severe chest pain while exercising. The patient, a Wall Street executive, fulfilled the frequent stereotypes applied to his profession, as he was impatient, aggressive, and fast talking. He claimed he was in excellent health and reinforced that self-perception by highlighting his regular intensive exercise regime. His stress test was halted when he presented electrocardiogram readings suggestive of coronary artery disease. JL was told that such a probable diagnosis could be confirmed and potentially treated using cardiac catheterization. Despite being highly educated and demonstrating substantial health literacy during the physician's consultation, he stated that he "didn't have time" for a procedure and that he was "in perfectly good health." He refused to consent to additional testing. He collapsed in the elevator when leaving the stress test appointment and then underwent an emergency procedure to insert a heart stent. Upon providing a more detailed account of his symptoms, the man admitted that he had been feeling chest pain and shortness of breath for several weeks and, with questioning, revealed a long family history of heart attacks among several male members of his immediate family including his father. He eventually admitted that he viewed heart disease as an unacceptable symbol of weakness and against the image he believed to be dominant in his profession.

- MJ, a seventy-two-year-old Haitian woman, accompanied by her forty-five-year-old daughter, arrived by emergency medical services at the emergency room after fainting. She complained of having experienced abdominal pain for four days. MJ appeared agitated and alternated between speaking creole and formal French. MJ did not speak English. The triage nurse attempted to attain her history, relying on her daughter to serve as her interpreter. In the presence of the ER physician, MJ began writhing in pain and had evidence of gastrointestinal bleeding. She was soon diagnosed with diverticulitis. When, still using her daughter as her interpreter, MJ was informed that she needed emergency abdominal surgery, both mother and daughter appeared panicked. That panic only worsened with the arrival of the surgical team, who immediately began telling MJ about the procedure and requested her consent without realizing that MJ did not speak English. Part of MJ's disjointed response were the words, "They never come back." Eventually, her daughter made it clear to the surgical team that MJ refused surgery. Some six hours later, with shift change, a Haitian nurse was assigned to MJ and was able to speak to her in creole. Not only was the nurse able to build trust and alleviate MJ's fears, but she also learned that MJ had lost two family members during abdominal surgeries. Indeed, a big part of MJ's willingness to put up with severe pain over the preceding days was rooted in a general fear of hospitals and medical procedures. Once the nurse was able to reassure MJ about the safety of the surgery and explain her fears to the surgical team, MJ agreed to treatment. She was discharged ten days later after a successful surgery.

Here are but three snapshots out of hundreds of millions. But what do they reveal? To answer that, we first have to consider how we define health equity. Here's how the Institute for Healthcare Improvement does: "Health equity is realized when each individual has a fair opportunity to achieve their full health potential."[6] It applies to access, treatment, and outcomes. To achieve equity in caring for patients means first they have to be seen as individuals. A humanistic approach to patients, something that is too often absent in contemporary medicine and traditionally not part of medical school training—is founded on the belief that "a patient is an individual to be cared for, not a medical condition to be treated." Our patients are our partners and have knowledge that is essential to their care. When the three snapshots are viewed through the patient as partner lens, we begin to see patients who are misunderstood, in denial, and who are fearful. Such emotions may be born out of culture or age, work environment, spirituality/religion, cultural values, personal beliefs, language, past experience or passed-on assumptions.

The diversity in these three examples is not grounded as much in the fact that they are Cuban American, White, and Haitian or even that they speak Spanish, English, and French creole. The most important diversity represented by their situations is that of having different health conditions, different perspectives, and different experiences prior to the medical encounters described. That they have different language needs or come from different cultures does matter, of course. Indeed, recognizing the needs and preconceptions of those realities is critical to their health outcomes, as is understanding all of their social determinants of health.[7] However, seeing each as an individual face within a larger mosaic of humanity is the essential first step on the pathway to each of them achieving their full health potential. And the second step on that pathway comes in recognizing that none of us can achieve our fullest human potential without our best possible health. For if the mosaic of Northwell Health employee faces offers snapshots of mothers and grandmothers and daughters, fathers and grandfathers and sons with genetic roots, near and far, stretching across the globe, they are but a reflection of the diversity of the community that Northwell Health serves and of our country as a whole.

REIGNITING THE HUMAN CONNECTION AND BUILDING A HEALTH EQUITY FRAMEWORK

To succeed in a twenty-first-century model of medical care delivery and take the steps necessary to coming closer to realizing health equity, we must see within the mosaic and recognize the individual faces. As healthcare professionals, we treat *people*. And as we grapple with ways to improve health outcomes, we must reignite this most personal part of healthcare and bring medicine back to its origins as the practice of human beings helping each other heal.

In the current American health system, if two people were to suffer the same acute health episode or be treated for the same

We have to meet patients in the moments and in patterns of their lives where we encounter them. Only then can we personalize their care.

chronic conditions, the likelihood is that that they would not receive identical treatment nor that they would encounter the same outcomes. This is true, no matter what demographics those two individuals represent. We have to meet patients in the moments and in patterns of their lives where we encounter them. Only then can we personalize their care. For it is through the human connection of treating individuals as individuals within the whole of what makes up their lives—their individual biology, background, history, family, beliefs, history, and the myriad other elements of what makes each of us human—that can move us toward the healthcare of the twenty-first century. It is beyond time that our humanity outpaces our technology and our medical knowledge.

This book will build an easily accessible framework for the incorporation of the tenets of diversity, inclusion, and equity into the healthcare tapestry. It focuses on reigniting human connections through empathetic, holistic, personalized health treatment, one where we view patients as partners. Such human connections as embodied in trusted patient/clinician/provider partnerships are foundational in establishing a pathway to diversity and equitable healthcare delivery. Our approach in this book builds on Northwell Health's ten-year journey of developing best practices in formalizing an approach to diversity, inclusion, and health equity and the many lessons we have learned while on that journey.

The three colleagues who serve as coauthors of this book—Dr. Jennifer Mieres, Dr. Elizabeth McCulloch, and Dr. Michael Wright—share the same collective mission, values, and dedication to fostering a culture of diversity and inclusion to achieve health equity. Our own pathways to Northwell are diverse.

Dr. Mieres is a cardiologist inspired to select her medical specialty by the death of her beloved grandfather when she was eight. Her day-to-day patient experiences compelled her to focus on disparities in women's cardiovascular health in an age when medical practice tried to treat women based on male physiology. Working so closely with women led to a dedication to patient-centered healthcare advocacy and developing the framework for the patient-as-a-partner approach, the development of four documentaries and two books on related subjects, a number of academic and administrative positions, and a natural course to becoming Northwell's first chief diversity and inclusion officer (CDIO).

Dr. McCulloch came to healthcare by way of a doctorate in social services that emphasized focus on gerontology and aging population health after developing expertise in statistical analysis of healthcare data and bridging the gap between data-driven research and developing human connections with the patients. Such expertise laid the groundwork for overseeing the establishment and growth of Northwell's system-wide language and communication-access services programs.

Dr. Wright arrived at Northwell after developing more than twenty-five years of business expertise in leadership development and implementation of business and talent strategies across corporations of global scale, linking that experience to academic research that includes a doctorate in education focused on business and organizational learning while also possessing a lifelong commitment to community leadership.

Drawing on our own personal backgrounds and our professional and academic expertise, we'll start by offering a holistic framework for diversity and addressing how we harness the value of diversity as integral in improving health outcomes in a global approach. And before we are done, we'll demonstrate how we have begun to pave a pathway forward to an expanded approach to healthcare delivery to include our patients as partners, crafting a truly personalized approach to medical care.

Ten years on, Northwell Health has succeeded in taking the lead in this space. We have systematically built a platform that has created powerful partnerships within our community and loyal allies throughout our health system in order to create an inclusive environment and remove barriers to equitable care. Where we started will be different than where you start. Our starting point was shaped in part by visionary leadership, by a rapidly expanding health system, by the development of a medical school that actively sought to develop humanism within its curriculum, and by having our roots in a community health system located in one of the most diverse places in the world. Through sharing our story, we hope to help you create or refine your own. For starters, we urge you to join us in holding a much broader, reframed vision of what diversity really is and why diversity and inclusion are so vital if we for the journey to health equity.

In *Reigniting the Human Connection*, we will share the approaches we have taken and the lessons we have learned in order to provide you the tools needed to implement practical solutions within your own organization. Each chapter opens with a brief snapshot of its focus to help guide your reading. And each of our "pillar" chapters ends with a template containing questions that can help you assess where you stand in the development of your own relevant structural approaches. The whole of that template is repeated at the end of the book and can provide an important tool as you inventory your organization's strengths and needs. It is our hope that you will exit the book with the knowledge you need to begin undertaking your own unique approach to embracing diversity, cultivating inclusion, and stepping closer to health equity for *all* of your patients. By appealing to your most human instincts, you'll find within these pages an essential framework you can adapt for your own journey. Your destination? To give each of your patients the opportunity to achieve their best possible health outcomes as they become partners alongside you in their care.

PART I

A MAP FOR ACCOMPLISHING NEEDED CHANGE

In Part I, we explore the terminology and applied principles of diversity, inclusion, and health equity. We then demonstrate how we have gone about creating a framework to move an organization forward on its journey toward health equity, including the application of the concepts of sustainable change management.

CHAPTER ONE

WHY A FORMALIZED APPROACH TO DIVERSITY, INCLUSION, AND HEALTH EQUITY IS MORE IMPORTANT THAN EVER BEFORE

Of all the forms of inequality, injustice in health care is the most shocking and inhumane.

—MARTIN LUTHER KING JR.

Recent events in social justice movements alongside the "catalyst" of COVID-19 have formed a "perfect storm" of opportunity for addressing diversity, inclusion, and health equity. Striking disparities in healthcare access and outcomes across diverse populations have entered public discourse in a way not seen before. Such awareness has created strengthened opportunities to develop highly structured, layered, and formalized approaches to take meaningful steps toward eliminating the presence of health inequities. Central to any formalized approach is recognizing the changing needs of twenty-first-century healthcare as systems shift to a holistic patient approach and learning to welcome patients as partners in their own care.

We live in an age when conscious or unconscious prejudicial actions based on race or gender, sexual identity, or disability or other differences that create marginalization are less likely to be overt and more likely to be systemic. Overt displays of aberrant behavior still exist of course—the too-common headlines of unwanted sexual advances by influential figures or widely publicized actions taken against marginalized people that inspire participation in social justice movements as immutable reminders—but in healthcare, we are more likely to see inequitable treatment in subtler measures. Subtle but real. We need to look no further than any number of alarming, disproportionate statistics among Blacks, Latinos, and Asians from the total population—unequal numbers of deaths and hospitalizations from COVID-19,[8] higher rates of chronic disease and premature death,[9] higher rates of preterm births,[10] slower and lower rates of inoculation for COVID-19[11]—to see we face disparities rooted in entrenched systemic causes.

A study conducted by the CDC in 2020 revealed life expectancy for Black Americans has lagged behind that of White Americans since 1950; indeed, the life expectancy of Black Americans in 2010 was equal to that of White Americans in 1980.[12] From 2019 to 2020, life expectancy for Black Americans declined by 3 percent.[13] This report is on data from January through June of 2020, and one of the conclusions reached by the authors of this study was: "Another consequence of the decreased life expectancy estimates observed during the first half of 2020 was a worsening of racial and ethnic mortality disparities. For example, the gap in life expectancy at birth between the non-Hispanic Black and White populations increased by 46% between 2019 and the first half of 2020 (from 4.1 to 6.0 years)."[14]

Systemic inequities don't grab the headlines in the way more overt prejudicial actions do. They tend to take the form of unconscious bias or historic employment practices that create an unlevel playing field or a one-size-fits-all approach to patients in medical settings.

The only way to battle systemic problems is through formalized approaches. Recent events, including the COVID-19 pandemic and wider support for social justice movements, reveal that a shift has occurred in the United States, and the general public is more aware of these systemic disparities. They are also more willing to support change that can end them, as public polls continue to show. This chapter will demonstrate both why enhanced awareness has created an increased need for action and what that has meant for the development of a formalized approach to diversity, inclusion, and health equity we have undertaken at Northwell Health.

Allow us to share a story that illustrates some realities of how disparities become systemic and that offers learning moments conveying many of the complexities that come with treating the whole person. This story emerges from a rather ordinary, even a happy medical event—the birth of a healthy child. Of course, even in a moment of bliss, we may encounter the unexpected if for no other reason than no two people are alike. In this incident, the birth of a male baby, while the family was in the midst of the euphoria experienced at the birth of a child, the attending medical personnel provided the new parents with a consent form for circumcision. The consent form— perhaps like the one used in your own health organization—was written in English, printed in tiny font, and filled with the necessary legal terms and medical descriptions. Enamored with their new baby, the parents signed without reading. Only later did the parents and providers alike come to fully understand the repercussions associated with signing the document. The parents' preferred language was not English. Even if they possessed greater comfort communicating in English, like most of those who work outside of healthcare occupations, it is uncertain that they possessed the health literacy required to understand all the form's details or legalese and ultimately make more informed decisions. To complicate matters, only after completing the procedure, medical personnel learned that the parents' cultural traditions had specific requirements for a ceremony to be performed during circumcision, something they regarded as an important rite crucial to establishing the child's identity and place of belonging in their religious community. Having the circumcision performed without holding this ceremony filled the family with heartache and held lasting ramifications for their child and his religious and cultural identity. By not having access to communication in their preferred language, none of the discussions took place that might have avoided this circumstance. Unable to converse, the clinicians had no way to know the cultural consequences of the procedure.

They had no intention to treat their patient with anything but the best clinical care possible. But they did, like all of us, possess unconscious cultural bias. The incident underscores the complex nature of diversity and the way in which negative outcomes can emerge from miscommunication, misunderstanding, and the assumptions that we all carry based on our experiences and upbringing, particularly in the high-stress, high-paced environment of a medical setting. And it illustrates how vital it is to treat every patient as an individual person. That's where reigniting human connections in healthcare starts, for inherent in such a value system is the recognition that health is everyone's most valuable asset.

In order to treat all patients as the unique humans that they are, we must first reframe how we think about several concepts, including far broader definitions of diversity, inclusion, and health equity, than most conventions apply. In the instance of this newborn, we not only failed to recognize the relationship between belief systems and health, but we also missed on another front, for we tripped on our first step in initiating a long-term relationship with a patient that can evolve over the continuum of their life span.

It has been well documented by numerous studies that only about 20 percent of a person's health is impacted directly by clinical care.[15] Because people spend nearly all of their time outside of medical encounters and because clinical care cannot impact health to the same degree as day-to-day living, 80 percent of our health is determined by things like access to healthcare services, socioeconomic status, physical environment, and lifestyle behaviors.[16]

The CDC defines social determinants of health as conditions in the places where people live, learn, work, and play that affect a wide range of health and quality-of life-risks and outcomes.[17] In plain terms, what we are really talking about is an individual's daily living.

If the child from the example above is raised in a neighborhood with frequent poor air quality, he's more likely to suffer respiratory problems. If his neighborhood has an abundance of full-service grocery stores, farmer's markets, or fresh produce stands and his parents have the financial means to put these resources to work, the child's health is more likely to benefit from balanced nutrition. When we consider these social determinants through the lens of a healthcare system rather than politics or sociology, it's not hard to see why it is that they have a disproportionate influence on an individual's health.

However, discrepancies in daily living are only exacerbated in a healthcare climate that has long focused on acute and chronic care, which is far more accessible to those with the economic and health insurance means to seek treatment. Historically, the medical community's metric for success was based on acute care. If a patient suffered a heart attack and went home after being treated in the hospital, the team felt that their job was done; they had saved a life. Part of what was missed with this model is found in what elements of that patient's lifestyle contributed to their overall health or their likelihood of suffering a heart attack. Also absent is what happens after they leave the hospital. Will they take prescribed medications? Will they attend follow-up appointments? Will they alter lifestyle patterns that will help them heal and that will help prevent another heart attack? Do they live in places or within cultures that will be supportive of their rehabilitation and care or support changes in behaviors? All these factors are critical to sustain the life "we saved" and to help, from a medical standpoint, to remove obstacles that can allow that patient the opportunity to achieve their healthiest life possible. In short, health doesn't begin or end after passing through the hospital's doors.

If we fail to consider the social determinants of health when we attempt to build a framework to address diversity, inclusion, and health equity, we are doomed to failure before we start.

If we fail to consider the social determinants of health when we attempt to build a framework to address diversity, inclusion, and health equity, we are doomed to failure before we start.

While twenty-first-century medical care is gradually doing more to address prevention and wellness, if we don't focus on the social determinants of health, we really can't help people achieve their best possible health. And once we do start to address such social determinants of health, there is no denying that the playing field is not level. We'll address that more in a moment. First, let's clarify what we mean when we use the terms *diversity, inclusion,* and *health equity.*

DEFINING DIVERSITY AND INCLUSION IN HEALTHCARE

Often when people hear the word *diversity,* particularly when it is formalized into the title of an office within a health organization, they think narrowly in terms of affirmative action or equal opportunity—the language of human resources. If they think more broadly than that, they are likely to see diversity only in racial terms. Things like hiring policies and other human resources concerns have an important place, as we will address when we focus on the workforce, but within human resource offices and beyond, diversity must be viewed with a more global lens.

Certainly, diversity importantly includes race and ethnicity, but if we are truly creating a healthcare environment where we treat the whole person, diversity also includes factors in an individual's life like gender; age; religion; mental health; educational level; sexual orientation or gender identity; cognitive, sensory, or physical disability; and geographic location. As we saw in the circumcision example, diversity includes the language a patient speaks, understands, and *prefers* and the cultural values that help define how that patient sees his or her world. And language does not convey the whole of culture. Cultural values might be formed primarily in the intimacy of your immediate family or shaped in part by national origin or by the influence of the cultural, religious, and business institutions in which we study, work, and practice our chosen faith.

DIVERSITY: The mosaic of people who bring a variety of backgrounds, styles, perspectives, values, and beliefs as assets to the workplace.

COMPONENTS FOR AN INCLUSIVE ORGANIZATIONAL CULTURE

Diversity focuses largely on the differences between people. Real diversity also means recognizing the variation that exists within groups rather than coldly slicing how we see people *into* groups. Here's a simple and useful way to recognize what we mean by the diversity that occurs within groups. Nearly every family has a favorite dish or recipe that's been passed down through the generations—the family favorite that fits our nostalgic taste buds. Maybe you remember your grandmother cooking this dish, and the fond memories of her get wrapped up in the taste and smell of that favorite food. Let's give your grandmother several sons-in-law and daughters-in-law, each of whom come from different backgrounds and different families but all of whom have come to cherish your grandmother's dish and now cook it themselves. Inevitably, each of their versions will taste slightly different. One is not better than the other, but each brings little bits of themselves—their own flavors and techniques, preferences and past experiences—to cooking. The output is no less delicious just because it is not an exact replica of what your grandmother cooked. That's a metaphor for diversity.

Our racial identities, cultures, ethnicities, gender, sexual identities, and physical abilities are critical parts of what makes us who we are, but so are all the other parts of our identity—our preference of sweet over savory, spice over bland—which is really to say our identities are also wrapped up in our passions and interests and occupations and habits. At some level, we all are diverse beings, not only in our ancestral past and biological makeup but also in things as ordinary as our taste buds and our preferences. All of us are altered by what we have experienced. Our diversity is part of what makes us unique. And for the medical professional, it's key that we recognize this full range of diversity within all the individuals we treat and with whom we work. Each person's unique nature also corresponds to improving their health outcomes. We care for people, not members of a particular category and not statistics of a diagnosed condition.

When we begin to see diversity as a mosaic of people who bring a variety of backgrounds, styles, perspectives, values, and beliefs—not unlike what we saw in the faces with which we opened the book—our communities and our workplaces become richer places. Twenty-first-century medicine requires an expanded healthcare delivery approach, one that is possible only with an expanded vision of what diversity means.

When we view diversity with an appreciation of individual attributes, we step toward inclusion. If we act on our desire to form human connections, we want to create environments, workplaces, and clinical settings where each person feels welcomed, respected, supported, and valued. This is true for our team members and for our patients. The individual differences that contribute to diversity are embraced. We see ourselves as stronger, more impactful, more flexible—more human—because of our collective differences. When we develop a supportive culture built on respect for others, it creates a pathway for individuals to do what they do best. When individuals apply their unique talents and abilities, processes improve, as does productivity. A wider variety of perspectives contributes to identifying more solutions more quickly. With more diverse solutions, patient outcomes improve.

When individuals feel valued within a culture of inclusion, they have a sense of belonging and feel part of a common purpose. In such a culture of mutual respect, we increase access to opportunity, build systems of equitable reward and recognition, and facilitate cultural competence. Imagine how improved patient outcomes can be when they enter a place where they feel understood and valued, where they see themselves as a respected partner in their own healing.

DIFFERENTIATING BETWEEN DISPARITY AND INEQUITY

For most of the history of medicine, we applied findings derived from studies of male anatomy and biology when diagnosing and treating women. We routinely treat immigrant populations without the benefit of medical histories. For patients without insurance or those without homes, medical care occurs in a patchwork of free clinics, emergency rooms, and health fairs, usually without coordination and often without record sharing. Consider four diverse groups frequently studied when developing data like life expectancy and other measures of health: women, immigrants, the homeless, and Blacks. Each group contains countless individuals with countless diverse medical needs. But have most health organizations developed a twenty-first-century approach that treats individualized medical needs? Have we constructed a healthcare environment where either unique biology or unique social determinants of health have been addressed? Nationally, have we evolved a healthcare system that supports equitable care? At Northwell Health, we are trying. While healthcare organizations alone do not have the power to improve all of the multiple social determinants of health for all of society, they do have the power to address disparities directly at the point of care and to impact many of the social determinants that create these disparities.

Health disparity is defined as the difference in health outcomes between groups within a population. While the terms may seem interchangeable, "health disparity" is different from "health inequity." "Health disparity" denotes differences, whether unjust or not. "Health inequity," on the other hand, denotes differences in health outcomes that are systematic, avoidable, and unjust. Further, the terms "equality" and "equity" are in no way interchangeable, as this illustration makes clear:

Equality

Equity

Source: © 2017 Robert Wood Johnson Foundation

Creating equity in healthcare is all about removing barriers and creating opportunities. But as the graphic makes clear, the ultimate solution to achieving the best possible health for everyone means doing away with the systems that erect barriers. This book, arising as it does from building our own systematic framework, is focused on identifying and creating the means to remove systematic, avoidable, and unjust barriers to achieving every individual's best possible health. Achieving health equity starts with communication, health literacy, and a culture of inclusion, humanism, and cultural sensitivity, connected then to research, education, and patient care.

"Health disparity" denotes differences, whether unjust or not. "Health inequity," on the other hand, denotes differences in health outcomes that are systematic, avoidable, and unjust.

HEALTH DISPARITY

Unjust differences in the incidence and prevalence of health conditions and health status between groups based on any of the following or a combination:

- Race/ethnicity
- Socioeconomic status
- Sexual orientation
- Gender
- Disability status
- Geographic location

HEALTH INEQUITY

Socioeconomic and systematic differences in conditions and processes that effectively determine health. Health inequities are avoidable, unjust, and therefore actionable.

- Unequal access to quality education, healthcare, housing, transportation, other resources (e.g., grocery stores, car seats)
- Unequal employment opportunities and pay/income
- Discrimination based upon social status / other factors

HEALTH INEQUITY IN THE AGE OF COVID-19

The presence of COVID-19 has made the presence of health inequity abundantly clear to a larger public and a more frequent conversation in healthcare circles. As the pandemic raged on, we began to hear the term "COVID catalyst" used because COVID-19 brought the issues of health disparities and inequities derived from social determinants to the forefront. Consider, for example, an individual who, in the eyes of health department policymakers, is defined when assessing community health needs during the pandemic as an "essential worker"—the clerk in your local grocery or convenience store. Such employees suddenly found themselves at the "frontlines" of maintaining a functional society and essential to sustaining overall public health. Most make only a dollar or two per hour more than minimum wage. A substantial percentage is held to part-time positions so that employers do not have to provide health insurance or other benefits. Nearly all are employed as shift workers, frequently working nights and weekends, and many are employed in businesses that are open twenty-four hours per day, which greatly complicates finding consistent childcare or attending to aging parents. Because they are low-wage earners, they frequently reside in substandard housing and often have lengthy commutes. Some of those commutes take place on public transportation in urban areas and are likely to involve long distances in rural ones. In the age of COVID-19, commuters on public transportation were in settings where it was difficult to maintain social distance, as were their work environments, which exposed them to near-constant public interactions in "high-touch" ecosystems. Is it any wonder that grocery store clerks were among the largest occupation to test positive for COVID-19? Given their working conditions and the socioeconomic realities of the United States, should we be surprised that people of color are overrepresented in these jobs?

By focusing on just one occupation impacted during the COVID-19 pandemic, we are provided a unique opportunity to look beyond statistics and focus instead on human lives. Think for a moment about the individual faces you see regularly. We don't know which clerk in our own local store suffers a medical condition that makes them more vulnerable to COVID-19 or asthma or who has an autoimmune disorder. We don't know which clerk goes home to a houseful of children or who tries to support a beloved elderly relative who lives in an assisted living facility. We don't know which are single mothers or who are students trying to pay for college. We don't know who has a second or third job elsewhere in order to pay their bills. We don't know who among these workers has health insurance provided by their employers. Yet during the pandemic, all were asked to continue working—to risk, literally, their lives—so that you and I could purchase food. There is so much we don't know about them. Sadly, we live in an age when if they do get sick, their healthcare provider likely could not tell us many details of their lives either and almost certainly very little beyond the clinical data that may—or may not—appear in their medical records.

Medicine in the twenty-first century must recognize that we treat the whole patient. And that means understanding their *individual* social determinants of health and their environment. Realizing this, at Northwell Health over the last ten years, we linked having a care team that understood the importance of diversity, health literacy, cultural competency, and other factors to our mission to improve health outcomes. COVID-19 wasn't an awakening for us, but it was an "aha moment" for why what we are trying to accomplish matters so greatly. Some of those grocery and convenience store workers died in our hospitals. They died alongside thousands of other essential workers, including far too many medical professionals. And some of those deaths would have been preventable if the disparities among diverse segments of the larger population didn't have such real repercussions.

THE HEALTHCARE JOURNEY IN THE TWENTY-FIRST CENTURY

Among communities of color, the inequality of access to and outcomes from healthcare have been studied and documented for decades. The facts were there for those who cared to admit their presence. COVID-19 presented us with an opportunity, for as awareness about healthcare inequities reached the mainstream media, they began to claw within the larger American consciousness. We reached, as we noted in the introduction, a syndemic. With or without the clarion call sounded by COVID-19, we are a country mired in an epidemic of chronic disease. That epidemic, like the pandemic, knows no barriers of economics, race, place, or culture. It can be mitigated by education and health literacy, but such access is currently unbalanced among socioeconomic, geographical, and racial divisions. The bulk of this book shares the systematic approaches we have taken to make diversity, inclusion, and health equity critical to our organizational mission to deliver equitable, patient-centered, quality healthcare.

But despite such a daunting landscape, we really do believe in the power of the human connection to create a more caring and just society. We can use COVID-19 as a catalyst for change to a truly twenty-first-century standard of healthcare for all.

Our experience also offers a reminder that the pathway to create medical settings that foster meaningful, sustainable inclusion and remove blockades that divide so many from achieving health equity is long. Our last ten years have been marked by purposeful, systematic steps. Those steps have led us to develop a formalized approach to creating sustainable diversity and inclusion, one that can provide an intentional algorithm capable of being incorporated into the healthcare delivery DNA. Every step has taught us a lesson. And those lessons have allowed us to embark on innovative approaches that can only arise from diverse minds coming together for a common purpose.

COMPONENTS TO ACHIEVING HEALTH EQUITY

HEALTH EQUITY = Elimination of Health Disparities

Patient Care

Social Determinants of Health

Health Care Team Education and Engagement

Research

Governance

Community

Diversity and Inclusion

Patient Education and Health Literacy

Cultural Awareness

Language Access

Humanism = Dignity and Respect

VISION: Improving the health and wellness of all communities served by Northwell Health

Leadership commitment | Education & development | Language access | Community partnerships | Workforce | Supplier diversity

Our mission is to advance the delivery of culturally inclusive health care and effective communication in partnership with our communities to achieve health equity.

STRATEGIC PARTNERS: Center for Learning and Innovation, Patient Experience, Clinical Service Lines, Health Solutions, Human Resources, Schools of Medicine and Nursing, Procurement, Quality, Feinstein Institutes for Medical Research, Katz Institute for Women's Health, Site Leadership, Ambulatory Services

THE RELATIONSHIP BETWEEN THE HUMAN CONNECTION, DIVERSITY, AND INCLUSION

Love is a combination of care, commitment, knowledge, responsibility, respect and trust.

—BELL HOOKS

All solutions to health inequities must be rooted in the material conditions in which those inequities thrive. To accomplish real change, we have to appeal to our best, our most human, nature. The hallmarks of the medical profession have always had their origins in humanism, and a return to a purer vision of what led all of us to healthcare in the first place will guide us to solutions. When we treat people as people and not as diagnoses or as representatives of groups, we enter an approach to care that can ensure everyone is treated with the dignity and respect they deserve.

Ten years into a journey aimed at achieving equity in healthcare for all who walk through the doors of Northwell Health facilities, we have often had to draw our own maps. Diversity, inclusion, and health equity remain largely new terrain for most. We've marked our routes. We've taken detailed notes. Sometimes the path forward has been filled with twists and turns and was often overgrown with dense underbrush. Part of that underbrush is formed by nearly continuous changes in approaches to healthcare because of new discoveries through research and care studies. Some has grown out of shifts in governmental regulation, changes to insurance policies, and alterations in funding models. And some of it is rooted in the less humanistic aspects of being human—the presence of bigotry, misogyny, and local, regional, and global tribalism, to name three. Though it requires hard work and commitment, such underbrush *can* be cleared. Along our journey, we have discovered many important segments of the path forward, and we've developed strong compass bearings that can help you find your way as well. We share our journey so that you can embark on your own.

The concepts that drive this book are many years in the making. For decades, women and members of marginalized groups in academic medicine have faced systemic problems such as racism, microaggressions, bias, harassment, heteronormative assumptions, disrespect, inadequate mentoring, salary inequities, and isolation, which have harmed their sense of belonging.[18] There has been substantial recent growth in important research examining these structural problems, but this book steps beyond identifying problems and is focused on presenting sustainable approaches to their solutions based on an awareness that "any solution to racial health inequities must be rooted in the material conditions in which those inequities thrive."[19] All the solutions we share with you in this book are carefully laid out in the pillars you encountered in the graphic that closed the last chapter. All have their foundations cemented in the belief that the human connection is foundational to achieving diversity, inclusion, and ultimately, health equity. Reigniting the human connections means paying attention to our best instincts, as President Lincoln alluded to in an 1861 speech when he said, "Though passion may have strained, it must not break our bonds of affection. The mystic chords of memory will swell when again touched, as surely they will be, by the better angels of our nature." When we listen to our better angels, we find a path forward.

Sometimes that's difficult. As medical professionals, we often face truly overwhelming and heartbreaking circumstances. Because that is true, we must build systems that support us during chaos. Consider the following story. At Northwell Health, we were at COVID-19's epicenter. One particularly heartbreaking but numbingly typical example of the individual toll of COVID-19 was shared with us tells of one specific patient. An Asian American small business owner in his fifties who could not catch his breath had been sick for several days and had put off seeking out care because past experiences led him to distrust the healthcare system. At admission, he was hypoxic and in need of oxygen therapy. Anxious, in physical distress, and wanting to return home and see his family, he continually removed his oxygen mask. While he was multilingual, like most of us when we are sick, we often revert to what is native, and this man's preferred language was not English. Yet the ominously, if necessarily, gowned and masked staff repeatedly pointed to the man's oxygen mask and, in English, tried to stress the importance of keeping it securely in place. Confused by the unfamiliar surroundings of a chaotic hospital swamped with patients, he continued to remove his oxygen mask with regularity over the course of the next two hours. Given the number of patients in similar distress, there was insufficient staff available to ensure that every patient was continuously monitored. The man went into cardiac arrest. Tragically, he didn't survive. Like all COVID-19 patients in severe medical need, alone among strangers in an ICU, he died when he may have had a different outcome had he arrived earlier or if he did not interrupt the oxygen treatment. Had someone communicated with him in his preferred language, might his life have been saved? Had we not been so inundated with patients, might a caregiver have been available to sit with him, to reassure him, to gently return his oxygen mask to its place? Questions like these haunt us. Healthcare providers are human, and the proximity to tragedy does not reduce its effects on them. Those who provide care to others suffer heartache as intensely as anyone. Such is the nature of being human.

Disease does not discriminate. It cares not about the suffering of the sick or for those who provide their care. It does not always adhere to statistics. It does not care that the man in the example we just shared, by being of Asian origin, had statistically less likelihood of dying than his Black or Hispanic neighbor. It did not differentiate when it sickened and killed so many of our colleagues who, like

Disease does not discriminate.

healthcare workers all over the world, joined the battle against COVID-19 rather than retreating from it, who went to work while so many of us were asked to stay home.

In such circumstances, how can we who have dedicated our lives to the medical professional not feel overwhelmed? The systems in which most of us were educated reminded us to focus on the biological and physiological elements of our training when emotion threatens to reduce our focus. Training in the healthcare sector, historically, has warned care providers not to become too closely attached to their patients. In a profession where tragedy and death are routinely present, there is the worry that their toll can tax providers and overwhelm them. And often, the thinking goes that if a caregiver becomes too personally involved in a patient's life, their judgment can become clouded by emotion, or they will be so overstressed that they cannot sustain their commitment to the profession and will burn out. We'd like to argue the opposite. If you fail to know your patients well—if you don't know about their living conditions, understand their support networks, have information about their lifestyles—you can't effectively heal them. If you can't speak with them in a language in which they are comfortable or recognize that they may possess cultural beliefs that make them hesitant to trust you, you cannot effectively communicate the needs of their conditions or create the best possible circumstances for them to fulfill their own role in their recovery. If we are unable to understand the human before us who has been placed into our care, how can we develop the synergy required to return them to good health?

Often patients feel alienated from their own care because the healthcare sector has increasingly become organizationally complex, bureaucratic, and highly dependent on sophisticated technologies, particularly in the latter decades of the twentieth century. As Dr. George E. Thibault notes in his editorial "Humanism in Medicine:

What Does It Mean and Why Is It More Important Than Ever?" there were a number of "dehumanizing" forces that moved medicine away from its humanitarian roots, including:

> the corporatization of the practice of medicine, the increasing role of business and finance in medicine, the fragmentation of patient experiences, the reduced time for clinical encounters, the increasing reliance on technology as a substitute for human interaction, and a de-emphasis on the humanities in the education of physicians.[20]

In short, the evolution of medicine over the past half century has made it an "increasingly analytic, biomedically focused field"[21] of study.

While Dr. Thibault's concerns remain dominant in contemporary medical practice, the behaviors of twenty-first-century *patients* have changed significantly, as have their demographics. For starters, we now live in an age where a world of medical information is instantly available just by reaching for our phones. Yet it can be nearly impossible for most patients to differentiate between what is legitimate information and what is nonsense, which points to another factor in the need for health literacy. But the upside is that we now operate in a climate where patients are more likely to approach their doctor with questions that originate from something they read on a website or in a social media feed. This shift is significant. We are not very far removed from when the predominant patient attitude was to wait and be told what would happen in order to "repair" them. Patients in the twenty-first century, often for better, sometimes for worse, simply have access to exponentially more medical information than at any time in the past.

The challenge now is channeling patients toward accurate, fact-based information among the daily slurry of open-source and competing layperson materials widely distributed in social media posts, blogs, and profit-driven advertisements camouflaged as health-related articles. We live in an age of clickbait. And among those trolling for our clicks is a vast flotilla baiting us with materials that supposedly hold answers through supplements, diet programs, fitness regimes, surgical procedures, and novel technologies to address our health questions. There is a plethora of quality medical information access available as well, but patients and consumers must be health literate in order to differentiate well-researched, evidence-based information developed by experts from the larger noise of media.

We need to remember why we became physicians and nurses and medical researchers in the first place. We, like you, chose careers in healthcare because we wished to make a difference in people's lives. How can we possibly recognize our patients' humanity if we fail to acknowledge our own? In the original Greek Hippocratic Oath and in all modern interpretations of it, humanism is everywhere present. The oath calls for physicians to recognize that their patients are sick human beings, not the symptoms of their diseases or the presentations of their injuries.

But how can the resurgence of human connections in a patient as partner relationship lead to better health outcomes? The first step is that connecting human to human helps us move past denial, whether that is denial within an individual about their own health condition or within a system about the presence of inequities. We cannot be successful in removing denial in either arena without improved health literacy. Often, we wrongfully assume that higher education is correlated with health literacy, yet when faced with illness, denial can prevail. Such denial speaks to the powerful reality that health literacy is dependent on the moment and on one's state of mind. A common phrase we use in our office is this: health literacy is a state, not a trait.

This recognition is why we encourage patients to never attend their healthcare appointments alone, to take detailed notes, ask questions, welcome the questions asked on their behalf by loved ones of the providers attending to them, and to seek out multiple opinions. Patients must become active agents in their own care. Unless they are, it is impossible to form patient/provider partnerships. Self-empowerment is a result of self-advocacy.

How do we define the humanism for which people like Marilyn Dienstag, the colleague to whom the book is dedicated, was such a staunch advocate? Here's one useful definition from Carol M. Chou, Katherine Kellom, and Judy A. Shea of the Perelman School of Medicine at the University of Pennsylvania. They define humanism in medicine as the combination of "scientific knowledge and skills with respectful, compassionate care that is sensitive to the values, autonomy, and cultural backgrounds of patients and their families."[22]

REIGNITING THE HUMAN CONNECTIONS IS ESSENTIAL TO A CHANGING HEALTHCARE LANDSCAPE

To understand fully why a human connection remains a necessary objective of twenty-first-century medicine, we must understand the nature of the system so in need of reignited human connections and the patterns by which we arrived here.

If we look across the past half century of healthcare in the United States, two primary patterns are revealed that are critical to understanding the transformation that is required to meet the needs of the present and future. Healthcare was once a paternalistic system where the physician was viewed as nearly godlike, and the domains of diagnosis and treatment were ruled exclusively by them. Patients and other medical professionals deferred to physicians' conclusions, seldom asked questions, and rarely confronted them. Doctors were placed at the center of a system that prioritized making them as efficient as possible. And while the majority listened to their patients and worked to relieve their patients' suffering, the premise was that the doctor was the key caregiver, so if the system could not maximize the utility of that doctor's time, we had designed a wasteful system.

You don't have to go far back in time to find a profession that was not only paternalistic but patriarchal, one overwhelmingly led by White male physicians. That reality has been slow to change. For example, in 2018, only 5 percent of physicians identified as Black, and 5.8 percent identified as Latino,[23] despite Blacks making up 13.4 percent of the US population and Latinos representing 18 percent.[24] And among physicians who are older, they are overwhelmingly male; in 2017, 69.5 percent of doctors between fifty-five and sixty-five were men. These patterns are changing, though far more by gender than by race. In 2017 those gender numbers seesawed, with 60.6 percent of doctors under thirty-five being women. However, communities of color remain severely underrepresented in the physician ranks. As recently as 2012, among practicing physicians, only 14 percent were Black or Hispanic.[25]

We'll go into depth later in the book about how impactful it can be for patients to have access to doctors who share similar life experiences or are of the same race or the same gender as their patients. The key takeaway at this juncture is that historically, because so much of medical information was concentrated in so few hands, patients seldom felt empowered and often regarded themselves at the mercy of their physician's expertise. Because health literacy remains low, many vestiges of this patriarchal system remain firmly in place.

A more diverse US population obviously translates to a more diverse patient population nearly everywhere across the country. This is strikingly true in all urban centers and in those rural areas where there is a historic concentration of migrant workers. Meanwhile, the organizational structures of the healthcare sector have undergone continuous change as well. Now doctors operate in medical teams. Long gone are the days of a single general practitioner who attended to your care from the cradle to the grave, referring you to specialists only when the medical circumstances were so specialized that they were beyond the abilities of a family practice. Today, not only are there medical specialists for every aspect of bodily function, but doctors of all specialties also are surrounded by substantial human and physical infrastructure. The physician remains as the lead in a medical team, but now most openly acknowledge their dependence on and the importance of a team made up of other professionals, including nurses, nurse practitioners, physical therapists, psychologists, nutritionists, and many, many others. Simultaneously, this team approach has been accompanied by ever-increasing specialization among physicians. The will to seek consultation from or referral to specialists had grown exponentially, which resulted in patients often seeing multiple doctors in pursuit of treatment and having fewer opportunities to forge closer, more personal relationships with any one physician. Twenty-first-century healthcare delivery is a team sport. The healthcare delivery model in this new century has expanded to say, "You're not alone."

Contrast that approach with the paternalistic nature of healthcare that existed for most of its history. Now we have the ability—if we have the will to follow our humanism and do so—to design the entire healthcare system around the needs of the patient at any given moment in their lives. We have the ability to determine who are the right people to satisfy that patient's needs, a view that is no longer physician centric. We can now assemble teams around the patient to address his or her medical issues in the most effective way.

While there are obvious medical advantages to having a large caregiving team where each member has specialized abilities, it's easy for patients to feel like a cog in the machine. All the more reason that all in healthcare must be intentional about being excellent communicators. That's also why the framework we have created at Northwell Health places the patient at its center. Without intentionality in creating a patient as partner approach, the very scale and complexity of modern team medical practice can fail, for no matter how talented the team and how advanced the science and technology, if the patient cannot understand their care regimen or does not feel heard and understood, they will feel like they have entered an alien, dehumanizing environment. We have to keep this patient-centric view at the forefront, for when do any of us feel more vulnerable, stressed, and isolated than when we are ill or injured? When are we in greater need of the human touch?

Recognizing the bureaucratic institutionalism present in late-twentieth-century medical practice, a leading advocate asking for medical professionals to remember the power of their humanity was Dr. Arnold Gold. A world-renowned pediatric neurologist at Columbia University's College of Physicians and Surgeons, Gold feared that burgeoning scientific discoveries and advances in technology were shifting the focus of medicine from caring for the whole person to an overreliance on technology. Dr. Gold believed that physician trainees were scientifically proficient and technically well trained but often demonstrated a sad lack of caring and compassion. To counter these trends, Gold and his wife started the Arnold Gold Foundation. The foundation focused on nurturing the tradition of the caring physician, a tradition that once epitomized most people's view of the physician as someone who knew you, your family, and your community intimately.

A VERY PERSONAL COMMITMENT TO FORMING HUMAN CONNECTIONS

Dr. Gold and those who now lead the Gold Foundation hold a vision of patient encounters that have great personal meaning for us and that echo our own foundational experiences. In Dr. Mieres's case, not only was she driven to healthcare by the childhood loss of her grandfather to a heart attack, but she also grew up on the island of Trinidad, where communities are extremely tight-knit, and people look after one another. Her father was a lawyer and a judge who was known and respected by his neighbors. People literally sought her father's counsel at their home any hour of the day. And if they had no means to pay her father, he would accept whatever they could provide, whether that was bags of tomatoes, mangoes, or eggs. Her father's actions taught his daughter that you never turn people away. The human connection as practiced in her home was about never turning your back on someone in need and providing them the dignity to pay for the services they sought through those things in which they placed value.

For Dr. McCulloch, while she ultimately became a strategist in the healthcare industry, she was introduced to the human connection of caring for others quite literally through Northwell Health. Throughout her childhood, she desired to be a medical doctor. One of the founding hospitals that would later become a flagship of the Northwell Health System was right in her backyard, and she spent countless hours volunteering there and seeing firsthand the role medical professionals played in the lives of their patients. There she witnessed a compassionate, person-to-person environment. Those impressions never left her, and as she continued her education, she learned that she could best serve the needs of others in her community by applying her skills to build programs to enable patients to be partners in their care. Through her expertise, she wanted to break down the barriers of viewing patients and their outcomes from a numerical standpoint by talking with patients and understanding the human connection in order to grasp why some medical approaches were working, and others were not. She has spent years bridging the gap between data-driven research and developing humanistic connections with the patients who supply such data.

Dr. Wright arrived at Northwell Health as the VP for learning at the Center for Learning and Innovation. He did so after holding similar positions at several global companies, something that might not have been predicted when, as a teenager in Canada, he trained with and volunteered for St. John Ambulance, which in Commonwealth countries provides services similar to what the Red Cross does in the United States. That core belief in helping others guided him toward preparation for the Roman Catholic priesthood, where, during his seminary training and professed religious life, he spent time working on psychiatric units and in young offenders' facilities, teaching and providing pastoral ministry. It was the values that drove him to such work and the importance he felt in working with people at such vulnerable moments of their lives that brought him to combine his expertise gained through leadership positions in large corporations to the desire to make change happen in a medical setting.

These are the personal drivers of our lives, commitments we hold to serving people that transcend jobs titles and cross the multiple layered systems and organizational structures of modern healthcare.

They are our roots. Through the belief that there is no greater impact we can have on another's life than helping them attain their best health, we have imagined the means to address healthcare disparities. In Gold Foundation research findings and initiatives, we have found approaches that parallel our philosophies. Gold Foundation approaches are echoed in the findings from a study conducted by Carol M. Chou, Katherine Kellom, and Judy A. Shea entitled "Attitudes and Habits of Highly Humanistic Physicians." Their study surveyed internal medicine residents at the University of Pennsylvania to find out which attending physicians they identified as role models. They then interviewed the physicians at the top of that list. Those interviews highlighted three significant traits of physicians who:

- approached patients with a sense of humility and real curiosity about their lives, especially toward those patients to whom it may seem difficult to relate;

- treated their patients as they themselves would wish to be treated; and

- saw their role as not merely taking care of the medical aspect of their patients but also helping their patients navigate through life challenges.[26]

THE PATIENT AS PARTNER

By practicing these humanist traits, physicians are one step closer to a key element of twenty-first-century medical care—seeing the patient as a partner. Patients live with their conditions every day and are experts when it comes to their own experiences of illness; this expertise should be welcomed, valued, and fostered by other members of the care team. In a patient-focused environment, patients are directly involved in shared decision making. This is critical because most of the day-to-day work of healing will actually be completed by the patient, such as following up with medical appointments; completing additional procedures; following discharge directives; taking required medicines; participating in physical, occupational, and other therapies that promote recovery; and following dietary and exercise advice. Patients need to have a hand in decision making because they will be the ones required to carry out the actions necessary for health improvement.

We have reached a place in the evolution of healthcare where we now acknowledge the eighty-twenty split we introduced in the last chapter—the fact that 80 percent of what drives an individual's total health is determined by life circumstances outside clinical care that can either nurture or impair health. Holistic care recognizes that no two lives are alike. A patient-centered partnership approach to healthcare promotes wellness and prevention.

The patient as partner approach is especially critical in the treatment of chronic disease. Take, for instance, the central role of behavior and partnership required for successful treatment for insulin diabetics. Not only must the patient monitor and regulate their insulin intake every day of their lives outside of immediate clinical oversight, but they also must be active participants in a regimen of proper nutritional balance and exercise. At the risk of oversimplifying these sorts of factors, ask yourself this question:

A patient-centered partnership approach to healthcare promotes wellness and prevention.

Which insulin diabetes patient is better positioned to manage their health—the patient who lives in an industrial center where poor air quality and frequent street violence forces them to spend most of their time indoors or the one who lives in a suburban neighborhood filled with safe, well-appointed parks, walking paths, and greenways? On this one measure alone, the answer is obvious. Building programs to meet the patient where they live in a way that accounts for diversity in access to participate in their care is where much of meaningful inclusion really starts.

Creating a culture of care is more complicated than simply reminding people of their original motivations to enter healthcare. Like all sustainable commitments to achieving health equity, it requires a systematic, intentional framework. How to go about developing such a framework is where we turn in the next chapter. The provider-patient relationship involves vulnerability and trust. It is one of the most moving and meaningful experiences shared by human beings. Our responsibility is not only to our patients but also to improving the systems in which we work—making care more reliable, accessible, equitable, and affordable for all the humans we serve.

CHAPTER THREE

A FRAMEWORK FOR DIVERSITY, INCLUSION, AND HEALTH EQUITY

*The true measure of any society can be found in
how it treats its most vulnerable members.*

—MAHATMA GANDHI

The United States has evolved into a multicultural society but has not evolved into one that affords consistent opportunities for economic, educational, or health gain for all its citizens. That reality has often created widely divergent communities that are sometimes in close proximity to one another but that have minimal interaction. It is human nature to have biases about ideas, people, and traditions to which we have not been directly exposed or with which we have intimate contact. With education, we can learn to face the unconscious bias we may hold. Once we do, we can see the positive health outcomes that accompany understanding our patient's language needs and cultural contexts, and we can recognize the value of forming inclusive partnerships with those in our care. To accomplish such transformation in thinking requires a systematic framework, one where the forces necessary to realizing inclusion and equity are identified, and specific structures are put in place to attain them. Building a systematic framework became a mechanism for making diversity, inclusion, and health equity a strategic imperative for Northwell Health.

It is the human connection that one sees in the smiling eyes that become the focal point of the mosaic we included in the introduction. The old cliché is that the eyes are the window to the soul. And if you look into the eyes of those healthcare workers working tirelessly to ease the fears and manage the symptoms of those suffering in Northwell Health ICUs during the peak of COVID-19, you will find compassion and empathy. Of course, in the age of COVID-19, those caring eyes were all that was visible, which offers a powerful visual reminder of the vulnerability patients feel in clinical settings and the fragility of the connection between them and their healthcare providers. It can be difficult to place trust in a stranger and more difficult still when you can't see their face.

But even when limited to reassurance offered through the warmth of eye contact, connection can be real. This is true because the traits of humanism are sincere and easy to find in those who dedicate their lives to helping others. Likewise, the foundations of an approach to achieving diversity and inclusion are built from approaches that recognize the power of the human-to-human encounter and originate in a desire to help others.

When mistakes in the care provided to a patient do happen, they are errors derived from another aspect of being human: imperfection. Sometimes we just don't know enough—medically, culturally, personally. Sometimes, in our human frailty, we feel crushed by the weight of impossible caseloads or beat by the exhaustion of seemingly never-ending shifts. And sometimes, we act upon the bias of which we are unconscious. Most bias begins with a lack of exposure. It's easier to hold uninformed bias about lifestyles that are different from our own, languages we do not speak or understand, and cultural beliefs we have not experienced. But of course, even unintentional errors remain errors, and unequal treatment of the people in our care cannot be excused. Both have very real medical and emotional consequences for our patients.

Certainly, as is the case among humans everywhere, within the medical profession, there are individuals who possess beliefs mired in racism, ageism, classism, and sexism, but they represent exceptions rather than norms. Even if they are a minority presence, such individuals have no place in our healthcare systems. We simply cannot tolerate beliefs that espouse inequitable treatment because of hate. But of course, we cannot remove such individuals from the healthcare industry until we eradicate the presence of hate in our society. That is a task far beyond the reach of any book.

But far more typical than extremist individuals who hold views formed by ignorance are the rest of us, who, with education and the proper framework, can learn to face unconscious bias we may hold, see the positive health outcomes that accompany understanding our patient's language needs and cultural contexts, and recognize the value of forming inclusive partnerships with those in our care. By developing offices within our healthcare organizations that are dedicated to educating workforces, forming alliances with partners in the community, and drawing on people's essential humanity, we can transform care in ways that have direct impacts on patient outcomes. To accomplish such goals requires a systematic framework, one where the forces necessary to realizing inclusion and equity are identified, and specific structures are put in place to attain them.

THE NATURE OF THE PROBLEMS THAT REQUIRE SYSTEMATIC TRANSFORMATION

First, we must understand the magnitude of the problem of inequity if we are to set about systematically transforming how we provide care and how we make certain that care is inclusive. A highly useful metaphor for illustrating social and health disparities is the "subway map" view of life expectancy, as expressed by Michael Marmot in his book *The Health Gap: The Challenge of an Unequal World*. Marmot draws on supporting data that illustrate how people's expected life span can largely be determined based on the neighborhood in which they reside as identified by a train or subway stop. For example, from midtown Manhattan to the South Bronx in New York City, life expectancy declines by ten years: six months for every minute on the subway. Similarly, between the Chicago Loop and the west side of the city, the difference in life expectancy is sixteen years.[27] As Dr. Daniel Berwick explains when considering Marmot's metaphor, "At a population level, no existing or conceivable medical intervention comes within an order of magnitude of the effect of place on health."[28] To put this in context, Marmot estimated if heart disease were eradicated for the entire US population, our country's life expectancy would increase by four years; this is barely 25 percent of the effect on life span associated with living in the richer parts of Chicago instead of the poorer ones.[29]

Consider, for illustrative purposes, a handful of disproportionate factors that contribute to weakened health for those who have little choice in their living environments and poor access to opportunities that could change their living conditions:

- compromised air because of proximity to manufacturing centers or congested urban traffic exhaust

- higher summer temperatures in urban heat islands

- lack of nutritional diversity, food access, or food affordability

- poor water quality because of outdated infrastructure

- shortage of public parks and clean, accessible open spaces

- unreliable sources of childcare

- increased exposure to violence

- increased distance from job centers and healthcare facilities

Now consider just some of what a pandemic has taught us regarding living environment and health: higher population density translates to greater difficulty to social distance; lack of financial resources means more difficulty in acquiring face masks, cleaning supplies, and other means of self-protection; dated rental properties and poor maintenance makes it unlikely to have advanced air exchange and filtration systems in homes and apartments; distance from work and retail districts creates dependence on the confined spaces of public transportation. Again, this list could grow much longer without much effort, but the point that emerges is obvious; we do not live in a country that provides equal opportunity for all. And that lack of opportunity has a direct translation to the quality of an individual's health and to shortening life span. In stark contrast, those who have the benefits of quality education, stable employment, safe homes and neighborhoods, and access to high-quality preventative services tend to be healthier throughout their lives and live longer. Of course, the measurement of mortality is but one data point for the health status of an individual or a population, but it is a powerfully illustrative one.

Solutions for healthcare inequity have to be conscious of these disparities made obvious by the pandemic, and they must be conscious of sociological and political realities that have created them, just as they have to know the history of the United States that has given rise to such unequal treatment. Drs. Rachel R. Hardeman, Eduardo M. Medina, and Rhea W. Boyd addressed this reality directly in a moving editorial for the *New England Journal of Medicine* when they wrote: "Any solution to racial health inequities must be rooted in the material conditions in which those inequities thrive. Therefore, we must insist that for the health of the Black community and, in turn, the health of the nation, we address the social, economic, political, legal, educational, and healthcare systems that maintain structural racism."[30]

As Dr. Donald Berwick so eloquently addressed in an opinion piece titled "The Moral Determinants of Health" in the *Journal of the American Medical Association*, because healthcare providers are committed to addressing the health problems of individual patients, "moral law" dictates that such a commitment, guided by science, must be logically extended to communal health as well.[31] He goes on to demonstrate that a goal of addressing the health problems of populations, not just individuals, requires healthcare professionals to fight on behalf of a whole host of human rights issues: for the preservation of authentically democratic systems, for addressing reform of criminal justice systems and climate change policies, and for recognizing the impacts of social determinants on health status. Berwick states that we must ensure "care for patients with illness and disease, no matter how they acquired their health conditions" and that we are morally obligated to address "toxic current social circumstances, including institutional racism, that make people—especially people of color and of lower income—become ill and injured in the first place."[32] We are in agreement with Dr. Berwick that taking such a humane and global vision of healthcare is required, that it is entirely "appropriate to expand the role of physicians and healthcare organizations into demanding and supporting societal reform." Indeed, accepting such an expanded role is the only means "for fixing the horrors of the subway map."[33] There simply exists no room for judging the humans we are tasked with healing. As so aptly

We must ensure "care for patients with illness and disease, no matter how they acquired their health conditions."

conveyed by peace activist William Sloane Coffin Jr., "Diversity may be the hardest thing for a society to live with, and perhaps the most dangerous thing for a society to be without."

A HISTORY THAT POSITIONED US TO DEVELOP A SYSTEMATIC FRAMEWORK

In order to discuss how you might best build a framework for diversity, inclusion, and health equity, it's useful to share a bit of the history of the one we have been building at Northwell Health over the past ten years. While our experiences will be different from your own, just as the needs of the community you serve are different than ours, the journey we have taken will prove instructive and can assist you in recognizing where you will find opportunities and where some of your greatest hurdles are likely to lie. Better understanding our journey will help you understand the processes and approaches we have put in place and the thinking behind them.

Partially that history is about some synergistic convergences, both within a rapidly growing Northwell Health system and in groundswell changes toward patient care and community health at the national level. Early in our journey, in 2011, The National Prevention Council, which had been formed through the passage of the Affordable Care Act the year prior, released its National Prevention Strategy aimed at increasing the numbers of Americans who are healthy at every stage of their lives by preventing injury and disease. The strategy also included:

> an important focus on those who are disproportionately burdened by poor health. In the United States, significant health disparities exist and these disparities are closely linked

with social, economic, and environmental disadvantage (e.g., lack of access to quality affordable healthcare, healthy food, safe opportunities for physical activity, and educational and employment opportunities).[34]

It focused on four "strategic directions" that remain central to our own systematic approach:

- healthy and safe community environments

- clinical and community preventative services

- empowered people

- elimination of health disparities

At the time of this writing, in 2021, the North Shore-LIJ Health System, renamed Northwell Health in 2015, now features twenty-three hospitals and over 750 outpatient facilities and has more than seventy-six thousand employees. The sheer scope of our growth and the diversity of the populations served by that growth has been critical to fueling the development of our strategy. Key developments to the growth and focus of the Center for the Equity of Care came in 2011 with the addition of the Zucker School of Medicine at Hofstra/Northwell and the Katz Institute for Women's Health, two institutions committed to meeting the changing needs and changing faces of twenty-first-century medicine.

Both institutions emerged in large part due to the visionary leadership of our CEO, Michael Dowling. Coming originally from an academic background in social policy and as a university administrator, he then held state government positions, including seven years as state director of Health, Education, and Human Services and several years as commissioner of the New York State Department of Social Services. His background provided a unique perspective on the needs of modern healthcare and shaped his abilities as one capable of guiding organizational transformation and igniting passion among his employees for a human-centered model of patient care.

The Zucker School of Medicine at Hofstra/Northwell turned traditional medical training on its head. In the words of its founding dean, Dr. Lawrence Smith, the philosophy behind this new medical school envisioned an approach to learning "where memory is not the gold standard but application and scientific concepts to real patients— knowledge and action as opposed to regurgitating facts."[35] After enduring an era when medical schools across the United States trained students within a litigious culture fraught with regulatory overreach that marginalized students in the care process, Smith, Dowling, and other colleagues sought to create a curriculum that changed this learning culture. In Dean Smith's words, "You can observe for the rest of your life, and you'll never become a physician. You have to learn by doing. At the Zucker School of Medicine at Hofstra/Northwell, we have pushed really hard to connect students with the patient and the community from the outset in a real role."[36] That early introduction to clinical medicine begins in the first week of medical school when incoming Zucker School of Medicine at Hofstra/Northwell medical students are placed with EMS teams so that their first steps into medical practice take place meeting patients in their homes and their communities at moments of a medical emergency. The work is face to face and hands on. It occurs in the environments where people live their lives and are surrounded by their loved ones.

Learning at the Zucker School of Medicine at Hofstra/Northwell means studying anatomy in cadaver labs where the donors' faces and limbs are visible, their identities and names are known, and their lives become real for students. It includes students keeping journals throughout the lab sessions and sharing the emotions they experience with one another as they reflect on the gift such donors and their families have made to their educations. A culture based on human connections means things like developing a literary magazine attached to the medical school, *Narrateur*, aimed at giving voice to the challenges and celebrations of patient care and to serve as a method of self-reflection. Such ideas are in line with the school's mission to train physicians who value professionalism, humanism, scholarship, and patient-centered care.

These and other elements were part of a culture and a curriculum designed to meet the needs of the community. They are similar to the formal recognition that women's biology is distinct from men's, and thus we needed a hospital dedicated to serving women through patient care and ongoing research. Such objectives resulted in the founding of the Katz Institute for Women's Health. These humanistic approaches used by both institutions shift the focus to putting patients first and actively teaching a holistic approach to healthcare designed to meet the individual needs of the patient.

It was that sort of vision and approach that defined Northwell's embrace of the National Prevention Strategy and guided the formation of a center dedicated to diversity and inclusion. It's the same vision that placed diversity and inclusion as central to the health system's mission, as reflected in making the chief diversity and inclusion officer a C-suite position in Northwell Health's leadership structure.

The team initially formed to populate what is now the Center for Equity of Care, Northwell Health's platform for diversity, inclusion, and health equity was small. We'll discuss more of its particulars and some of its experiences in the next chapter when we focus on the role of leadership as a fundamental pillar of the strategic framework for promoting equity, but the significant progress Northwell Health has made on achieving a diverse and inclusive environment would not have been possible without a dedicated center. The formation of such an initiative is part of a purposeful approach that Northwell saw as central to its commitment to the goals of the National Prevention Strategy.

WHERE TO START?

We started out with a blank slate. Our hope is that sharing our experience means you won't have to do the same. In our case, ten years ago, there were very few health organizations that offered any sort of pathway we might follow. Where we found good ones that established best practices, we followed them and built upon them. One such source of best practices was found in the thought leadership provided by Dr. Joseph Betancourt through Massachusetts General Hospital Disparities Solution Center. Dr. Betancourt and his colleagues at Massachusetts General Hospital Disparities Solution Center laid out a vision of best practices. Several echo the needs we identified as we began to formulate our pillars for equitable care. Among others, they argued for the following "recommendations for addressing and eliminating racial/ethnic disparities in healthcare:

- Increase the entire healthcare team's awareness of racial/ethnic disparities.

- Improve care systems by collecting data on patient REAL, improving quality, using evidence-based guidelines and multidisciplinary teams, reaching out to the community.

- Facilitate interpretation services to address language barriers in the clinical encounter.

- Educate the entire healthcare team on health disparities, cultural competence, and the impact of race/ethnicity on clinical decision making.

- Empower patients to be more active in the clinical encounter and more effectively navigate the healthcare system."[37]

Massachusetts General Hospital Disparities Solution Center has also provided substantial research on some of the initiatives needed to meet these and similar recommendations. They identify three simple steps that hospitals can follow to ensure more comprehensive care that parallel our own beliefs. These offer an excellent starting point for systems that are in the early stages of developing diversity and inclusion programs:

- Creating a strategic plan that follows the Institute of Medicine recommendations and focuses on collecting key demographics, measures quality performance, then identifies gaps in quality and develops interventions to meet them.

- Training staff in cross-culture care by promoting a continuous learning atmosphere that focuses on cross-cultural care and communication and that stays up to date on the latest research findings related to racial and ethnic disparities.

- Monitoring and measuring performance. Publish findings annually that are made readily accessible to the public. From such measurements, you can then create programs to eliminate disparities.[38]

Among the very first steps taken by our office was to determine where we actually stood in regard to our approach to diverse patient populations. How did we measure up against the National Prevention Strategy benchmarks? The general critique of Northwell Health when we started out was, particularly in the recognition that we served such a notably diverse population, that we needed to align with the curriculum of our what was our fledgling medical school. In short, how would we educate our students to serve our diverse patient population if we did not address our shortcomings as an existing health system?

What we believed from the start was that diversity and equity needed to be linked to patient outcomes. We knew we had to focus on more than acute care, for that had accounted for many of the shortcomings of a national healthcare system struggling to adjust to the needs of a new century. For decades nearly all in healthcare had poured resources into managing acute care without examining the causes of many conditions and diseases or shifting toward an approach of disease prevention. How might we develop a strategy that considered our patients' access to care and that took into account their culture, language, and health literacy? We understood that we had to help fashion a healthcare team that could develop competencies in these three areas, or we could never fulfill our mandate of improving health outcomes. So among our very first steps, we set about analyzing a patient satisfaction survey as one important measurement to determine how our health system was seen by those using it.

The results were revealing, and they not only helped us establish our priorities in moving forward, but they also gave us preliminary data to place within the context of the National Prevention Strategy and within the findings of those doing relevant research. Over time we were able to articulate the major pillars of a strategy required to meet our objectives. Those have been refined and revisited in the years since, but they gave us a path to begin walking.

THE PILLARS FOR ESTABLISHING A FRAMEWORK FOR DIVERSITY, INCLUSION, AND HEALTH EQUITY

What does the framework that emerged from our commitment to improving the health of *all* of our patients, at every stage of their lives, look like? A holistic approach to diversity, inclusion, and health equity in healthcare includes a framework that extends beyond the focus on patient outcomes to include equity in numerous other ways to include supplier diversity, employee resource groups, and community partnerships. We have developed the following foundational "pillars," all aligned in order to provide a comprehensive, strategic approach to transformation. Each pillar represents an essential component for accomplishing safe, quality patient care capable of meeting the diverse needs of patients and grounded in the concepts of the human connection in healthcare.

VISION: Improving the health and wellness of all communities served by Northwell Health

| Leadership commitment | Education & development | Language access | Community partnerships | Workforce | Supplier diversity |

Our mission is to advance the delivery of culturally inclusive health care and effective communication in partnership with our communities to achieve health equity.

STRATEGIC PARTNERS: Center for Learning and Innovation, Patient Experience, Clinical Service Lines, Health Solutions, Human Resources, Schools of Medicine and Nursing, Procurement, Quality, Feinstein Institutes for Medical Research, Katz Institute for Women's Health, Site Leadership, Ambulatory Services

- **Leadership commitment.** Encourage and cultivate strong leaders in diversity, inclusion, and health equity. Without the active support of leadership at every level or absent an intentional governance structure, none of the other objectives are achievable. Leaders must be authentic in their humanism and mindful of wanting the highest achievable outcomes for every patient. Those focused on diversity and inclusion initiatives must have a direct channel of access to senior management.

- **Education and development.** If patients cannot understand what their healthcare providers are telling them, they have no reason to place trust in us and no means to become partners in their care. A great deal of inequitable medical treatment is caused by failures in communication or the inability to consider cultural values.

- **Language access.** Ensure that patients have rapid, reliable, interactive access to information provided in their preferred language. Language access must be provided in all encounters with the health organization, in person, remotely, in print, and in digital interactions. Great language access programs go beyond communication in the patient's preferred language and incorporate other education approaches that make certain communication is provided in a health-literate manner as well.

- **Community partnerships.** Eighty percent of what accounts for a patient's total health is determined outside of clinical settings in the places they live, learn, work, recreate, and worship, so we must develop and sustain effective community partnerships. If we fail to extend clinical care into the larger communities we serve, we'll never improve our patients'—our neighbors'—health.

- **Workforce.** We must recruit and support a diverse workforce. Patients will become better partners in their own care and do so in an environment where they feel trusted and understood if the workforce of the healthcare system represents the diversity of the patient population.

- **Supplier diversity.** Fostering economic viability in our communities by doing business with those that reflect our community. Because our patients, like our colleagues, really are our neighbors, we have to contribute directly to our communities by creating economic interdependencies and forming alliances with the businesses and organizations in our own backyards.

These six pillars are united by a mission to create and sustain a culture of inclusion in every aspect of the system that can, directly or indirectly, impact the nature of patient care. The goal is to create seamlessness in the presence of human connections across all parts of the health system. All the pillars are grounded in a philosophy of developing relationships of mutual trust by making sure that patients feel respected, understood, and heard.

The six chapters in Part II of the book develop each of these pillars in depth and explore how we have approached making such goals attainable and become part of our core culture and our day-to-day operations. There is no hierarchy in the importance among the six, and each must work with the others to accomplish the aim of achieving health equity for all.

All six pillars share recognition in their foundational architecture that workplace cultures really do take on the personalities and priorities of those who work in them. In essence, the caring, smiling eyes of the mosaic we referenced at the outset of this chapter reflect the humanism of the Northwell Health team and the culture it has tried to establish. In those eyes, we find medical professionals who feel driven to help others. Acting on that drive is made easier and is more fulfilling because they work in a setting where there has been a conscious effort to prioritize care that is compassionate and inclusive, one where the standard is to try and have all encounters feel personal. Did we get it right every time with every patient experience? Of course not. But we are diligent as a team in holding ourselves to the highest standards of holistic patient care, are willing to admit when we fall short, and are intentional about learning from our mistakes.

Arriving at the sort of workplace culture that reflects the best of its humanism requires a great deal of work, nurturance, and infrastructure. It requires changes in systems and attitudes alike. It demands that all see themselves as working toward common objectives. None of these are easy tasks. They certainly don't happen simply by wishing for change. To fully reestablish human connections and accomplish real transformation, you must develop a systematized methodology of change management, which is the focus of the next chapter.

CHAPTER FOUR

CREATING A FRAMEWORK FOR SUSTAINABLE CHANGE

Progress is impossible without change. And those who cannot change their minds cannot change anything.

—GEORGE BERNARD SHAW

Healthcare systems have shared in an inhumane national history, sometimes openly and more often through systemic differential and deferential treatment of the very people with the greatest need of care. Responding to the systemic inequality that has resulted from that history requires the intentional application of quality, system-wide change management practices so that all stakeholders see diversity and inclusion as a fundamental commitment. Those invested in leading healthcare institutions toward greater diversity and more inclusive practices have to be knowledgeable in designing and sustaining effective change management strategies.

The tasks before us are staggering. The United States is a nation of immigrants, yet one stained forever by its participation in the anathema of slavery and by its near extermination of its indigenous peoples. While many would argue, ourselves among them, that it is the diversity of its international immigrant population—this hearty, enrichening gumbo stew of culture and ethnicity, race, and experience—that is America's single greatest asset, it is a history repeatedly marred by treating the most recent immigrants to reach its shores as less than human. This abhorrent history of unequal justice—not just for Black and Brown people but for LGBQTIA+, the disabled, veterans, women—is historically present in all of our institutions. Too often, those institutions have been complicit in sustaining unjust treatment. Healthcare systems have shared in that inhumane history, sometimes openly and more often through systemic differential and deferential treatment of the very people with the greatest need of care. As a nation, we have inched toward equality, but it remains a halting and unpredictable movement forward. The need for change is overwhelming and omnipresent.

Additionally, there is an urgency to expanding the healthcare delivery system to improve health outcomes for the epidemic of chronic diseases. Building a framework that integrates the components of diversity, culture, and language into the healthcare delivery system is essential for customized patient care.

We hope the preceding chapters have established this need for change. We have also introduced the central tenets of twenty-first-century medicine that can help us change the imbalances that exist. But to accomplish the objective of achieving health equity, we all must become agents of change. The stakes could not be higher. So how do we go about tackling change that is so great in scale and complexity? Part of the answer resides in applying the principles of change management. It starts by explaining our "why." Our why is straightforward: human beings are human beings; all humans deserve to be treated fairly and with respect and are entitled to lead the healthiest lives possible.

In the book that launched Simon Sinek as a central figure in leadership theory, *Start with Why: How Great Leaders Inspire Everyone to Take Action*, he introduced his model of the "Golden Circle." In short, the Golden Circle concept posits that people and organizations, whether trying to sell a product or lead a change, start from the outside a circle and work their way in when explaining their approach; they start with *what* they do (what an organization does or sells), then share *how* they do it (what sets the organization apart from others), and if they get to it at all, they end by addressing *why* they do it (what is the purpose, cause, or belief guiding the organization's actions). Sinek suggests that the people and organizations that are able to inspire others and differentiate themselves succeed because they operate with transparency and start by explaining *why* they do what they do. This is the approach famously taken by Apple. Apple doesn't really sell you a laptop or a phone (the what); they sell you a belief that the company challenges the status quo by thinking differently (the why). The neuroscience behind the Golden Circle theory is that humans respond

The people and organizations that are able to inspire others and differentiate themselves succeed because they operate with transparency and start by explaining why *they do what they do.*

best when messages communicate with those parts of their brain—the limbic brain—that control emotions, behaviors, and decision making.

To further explain, Sinek reminds us that while Martin Luther King Jr. was a gifted orator, he certainly was not the only passionate, committed, capable civil rights leader of his era. What differentiated King, Sinek suggests, is that he started with why. He appealed to people's emotions. Because he succeeded in sharing what he *believed*, he reached those who shared his beliefs. Sinek jokes in a TED talk about the Golden Circle that when King addressed the crowd at the March on Washington for Jobs and Freedom in 1963, his speech was titled "I Have a Dream," not "I Have a Plan."

Like Martin Luther King Jr., if we are to be successful in moving an entire system from a patriarchal history that produced unequal care for different patient populations to one that provides equity of care for all, we are going to have to share our "why." We have to be willing to demonstrate the passion and sincerity of our belief in King's statement, "Of all the forms of inequality, injustice in health care is the most shocking and inhumane," and we have to successfully help all the stakeholders we serve see why that belief matters to *them* and to the larger organization. We must create a compelling reason so that people want to contribute to change. Our approach at Northwell Health has been to try and help others see how the need for change and our specific strategy for accomplishing it connects to what they do each and every day. We have found that it is insufficient to focus on the process of change or the structural aspects of change alone. If people cannot see why change matters in their own lives, they will never be able to move on to the *how* and the *what*.

An important part of how we articulate the why for others is through storytelling. Stories that emerge from real people's lives allow us to appeal to stakeholders' emotions and reach that limbic part of the brain that makes them want to change their behavior. In the spirit of storytelling, consider this one.

Kathy was a forty-nine-year-old empty nester who, after years of neglecting her health, became determined to change. Alarmed by feeling fatigued and suffering a decreased exercise capacity, she scheduled an appointment for a thorough physical. Her doctor, acceding to the expectations of a system that emphasizes diagnose/treat/release, performed an EKG, which came back normal. Despite her protests, he dismissed her family history of heart disease, told her she was fine, and said that she simply needed to lose weight. He recommended no further action, offered no insight on how to achieve weight loss, and scheduled no follow-up. Sound familiar? This has been the typical pattern of patient/ physician interaction for decades. It is quite likely that her doctor, as he moved on to the next patient, exited her exam feeling he had done exactly what was expected of him by running a diagnostic test. Was there any reason he would so much as think about Kathy tomorrow?

Not satisfied with the advice to "lose weight" and concerned about a family history of cardiac disease, Kathy consulted a cardiologist specializing in women's heart health, who, instead of dismissing Kathy's concerns, did something else: she listened. She considered Kathy's family history, ethnicity, and health phobias and ordered another exam of Kathy's heart. This time, the test showed Kathy had nonobstructive coronary artery disease. The physician then engaged Kathy as a healthcare partner, and together they created a heart-healthy living plan that was realistic for Kathy's social determinants of health. It included lifestyle changes and medication to control her blood pressure. She referred Kathy to a nutritionist and advised her to take up yoga. Soon, Kathy was losing weight and getting in shape to lower her heart attack risk. The approach benefited both Kathy's health and the system's bottom line. Open-heart surgery is costly and requires a long recovery period and prolonged hospitalization. Controlling heart disease risk factors and avoiding surgery with medication, exercise, and portion control is certainly less expensive and less traumatic. The test run by this second doctor wasn't different, even if its results were. That's not the story. The story that mattered was that Kathy's doctor listened to her concerns and investigated further. Then she tailored treatment in a manner that brought Kathy and her day-to-day realities into the plan. They became partners for achieving better health.

This shift in approach to Kathy's healthcare will sound familiar, for it is the central theme of this book. But what we can't look past are two realities it exposes: (1) what Kathy experienced with the first physician is the overwhelming norm not only in how most healthcare interactions proceed, but it also is an extension of how we have educated health professionals for most of the last one hundred years, and (2) what can seem a fairly simple shift in approach had a profound transformation in Kathy's health and her prognosis; Kathy wasn't just made healthier by making her a partner, but her life also became fuller, and she felt in control of her own body rather than a cog in a bureaucratic healthcare machine.

Why is Kathy's story relevant to the topic of this chapter—change management? Because Kathy, while very much one flesh and blood human with a single unique history and set of experiences, is representative of millions of other women. Her personality may be unique, facets of her biology may be distinctive, but her medical care prior to this second consultation was not. As a set of biological data, Kathy's story is ordinary to the point of invisibility. As a human, Kathy has a story that is rich, diverse, and specific.

In order to achieve health equity for all, we're not just talking about lip service variety of opening more doors to more people; we must overhaul essential elements of healthcare culture. We must fundamentally ask, "How do we treat patients?" If we do not concentrate on what

If we do not concentrate on what actions, behaviors, lifestyles, habits, resources, and inequities make up our patients' lives after they leave our examination rooms, we cannot truly move them to the best possible outcomes.

actions, behaviors, lifestyles, habits, resources, and inequities make up our patients' lives after they leave our examination rooms, we cannot truly move them to the best possible outcomes. Nor can we end health injustice. To accomplish both aims, we have to transform the essential constructs on which much of healthcare has been built. This is no insignificant transformation. Everything we have written about the need to shift to holistic healthcare is repeated in the challenges of creating true diversity and inclusion in healthcare systems. Moreover, the two are inextricably linked.

Change is difficult. Dr. Martin Luther King Jr. captured this powerfully when he said, "Change does not roll in on the wheels of inevitability, but comes through continuous struggle." Yet change we must.

THE JOURNEY OF CHANGE

When we started on our journey to create the systematic framework that we have shared with you, there was a lack of recognition and understanding of the true meaning of diversity and its role in the healthcare world. If employees were encouraged to contribute potluck dishes reflective of their ethnicity, surely that was sufficient to reflect a diverse workplace. We've come a long way, but we've got a long way to go. To transform a long-established system to one of holistic patient care requires a sea change that seeps into every aspect of the patient experience, one that recognizes the full context of diverse human populations. That won't be accomplished by asking that clinicians consider their "bedside manner," nor with more potluck dinners (although there's a place for sharing good food with coworkers!).

Such a scale of change is extraordinarily demanding and not easily accomplished. But then Kathy's personal change wasn't easily realized either. The lifestyle change required to improve her health required overturning a lot of lifelong habits and finding mechanisms to overcome limits presented by her external circumstances. Anyone who has tried to lose weight knows that simply saying that you will watch what you eat won't cut it. You need help. You need accountability. You need an action plan. You need good role models and partners and new recipes, new grocery store habits, good advisors, and a purposeful routine. And still, it will be hard, even if you are truly committed. There is a direct correlation between all these approaches to weight loss and those required by change management in business.

Like the difficulty Kathy faced to change her habits, her first doctor must be willing to make hard changes as well. That's difficult, for he, like his peers, is acting upon years of training and decades practicing within a system that reinforces that training. Systems of care, historically devoted to the treatment and prevention of infectious diseases amid discrete episodes of acute care, are now increasingly occupied with the management of chronic health conditions. That influences a diagnosis/treatment approach. Moreover, the sheer number of journal articles, technology assessments, and practice guidelines that any provider must read to stay current is now well beyond human capacity.[39] It is easy, therefore, for healthcare professionals like Kathy's original doctor to think they can't possibly take on one more demand.

Yet the reality is quite the opposite. Holistic healthcare provides clinicians a partner. If we can learn to frame people's health in the proper context, they'll see that they have the power to better their lives by bettering their health and that no one has a more vested interest in doing so. Ask anyone in any profession: having a motivated, invested partner who is willing to learn makes any job easier. For both Kathy and her first doctor, convention is all that they had ever known. To step out of what we know is never easy. In the twenty-first century, we now ask doctors to understand their patients' environments and social determinants. It can feel like an overwhelming demand for many.

Think how often over the course of a physician's career she is asked to master a newly developed surgical technique or incorporate a nascent technology? How often has he had to learn about the interaction risks and side effects of new pharmaceuticals or adjust to research that has challenged the efficacy of once-accepted treatment approaches? Doctors are no different than their patients when they must relearn what they thought they knew as research uncovers new evidence. Consider a familiar example: it may be true that there are plenty of diet fads or weight loss regimens that become the "it" topic each year, but just as often, researchers really have unearthed new data on what constitutes a healthy diet that considers an individual's unique biology; this can seem like shifting or even contradictory medical advice. In reality, it's simply an example of how healthcare can move forward with new information. This is equally true for what we now know of the complex interactions between chronic disease and ancestry, reactions to viruses and race, and posttreatment follow-up and economic stability, to name three growing bodies of medical research. Health professionals are accustomed to change demanded by a profession that is constantly driven forward by academic research and improved technology. While some in healthcare have been slow in adjusting to the more human dimensions of patient care needs, they are quite capable of change.

CREATING STRUCTURE FOR CHANGE

It must be said, however, change must be structured and supported. Just like Kathy's personal change, cultural change in an organization only works when it is intentional. There has to be a cohesive strategy that clarifies the objectives and the methods for accomplishing them, and everyone must participate.

Change will be demanding, and it must occur with an awareness of the human factor. A great deal of successful change in any organizational setting—and in individuals, including in regard to their health—is attributable to human behavior. Consider this finding from the Institute of Medicine Committee on Health and Behavior: Research, Practice, and Policy:

> *Behavior can be changed: behavioral interventions can successfully teach new behaviors and attenuate risky behaviors. Maintaining behavior change over time, however, is a greater challenge. Short-term changes in behavior are encouraging, but improved health outcomes will often require prolonged interventions and lengthy follow-up protocols.*[40]

What's true when it comes to human health behavior, like smoking cessation or diet programs under the supervision of a physician, is also essentially true of the organizations in which physicians work. It is imperative that the needed change is communicated in human terms tied to holistic health and patient outcomes. For starters, if we want a change from medical professionals, we must address why the change is necessary. We must anticipate and answer questions such as the following: How will a doctor's or a nurse's life be made easier? How might change contribute to better patient outcomes? What's in it for the organization? What would happen if we didn't change? What's the business rationale for this change? If individuals or entities recognize that change is desirable or improves their ability to complete their mission, then there is the desire to change. To ensure sustainable behavioral health changes, the steps in transition will need to be incremental, the change protocols will need to be clearly communicated, and desired behaviors will need to be repeatedly reinforced. What you've seen in trying to accomplish change for patients you treat will apply to systemic change as well.

Once we have addressed the questions stakeholders will have, then those stakeholders must be provided the tools to educate patients on why change matters. Those in the medical profession ultimately want to make their patients healthier—that's their instinct for human connection. Therefore, as in any partnership, clear communication of data and shared decision making is important in adherence to a treatment plan.

Change at an institutional scale cannot take place without a thoughtful framework. This is why we have been so purposeful in developing the foundational pillars that form our approach. Each must be developed in a strategic manner in partnership with stakeholders if we are to accomplish change, and our experiences with conducting change management are threaded through every chapter.

That change cannot be accomplished without the pillar with which we start: strong leaders. We will speak in the next chapter about the importance of having strong central leadership that supports diversity and inclusion and is vocal about that support with their words, actions, and finances. But here, let's focus on the need for leadership competency.

In another aspect of what has traditionally been a paternalistic approach in healthcare, much of its leadership arises out of the physician ranks. An excellent physician or outstanding nurse does not automatically make for a good leader. Just as you had to learn how to be a strong medical practitioner, you have to learn to become a strong leader. This is best accomplished by incremental advancement supported by ongoing education, something that should be considered as you develop your leadership team for diversity and inclusion. New or prospective leaders or those in charge of expanding programs in the diversity and inclusion space should be encouraged to seek out, or better yet, be provided, leadership education. Strong leadership development systems will encourage providing newly hired leaders with experienced mentors as an ongoing resource. New leaders will need advice from those who are experienced at managing people and shepherding new policies and procedures in large organizations. All of this should be in addition to taking seminars, attending workshops, and reading books that expose you to the advice of leadership experts.

By seeking out experts and requesting more education, one can be better positioned to demonstrate key qualities of effective leaders, such as consistently acting with integrity, self-awareness, gratitude, respect, and empathy. One will learn how to be agile and adaptable, how to delegate, and how to capitalize on your influence, harness your powers of persuasion, and recognize when to show courage. As a leader, you'll be expected to craft a vision. You will learn to draw on the efforts of those around you to define and articulate this vision, and you will be reminded to give them credit to the point that you step back and push them forward. You will recognize the importance of belief in the vision and demonstrate that belief to others. The vision you develop must be succinct. Practice your elevator pitches, for if you can't give what feels like a comprehensive expression for the why and the what in a five-minute session with a stakeholder, you may struggle to bring them on board as an ally. And chief among all the skills you will need, you'll learn tools for being an effective communicator who understands how to engage others with messages that are critical to the work of the team you lead and the objectives required to best serve your patients and employees.

If you can succeed in integrating these characteristics and making them a genuine part of how you approach all of your responsibilities, people will *want* to help you coarchitect and be involved in this change. Only then will you receive the buy-in and commitment needed. These are cultivated characteristics. They will take time to learn, and you will never master them. But if you are honest with others when you fall short, and you demand a high bar of yourself, people around you will respond, and you will create a culture where people are committed rather than compliant. This is a culture where change can occur, for people throughout the organization will see themselves as your partners.

To capture commitment, you will also need to be intentional in cultivating relationships with all the stakeholders in your organization. Without involving them in the change design and implementation, you will risk losing sight of critical perspectives and may cause resistance. You need their support. This is where past education and experience in presenting medical research to colleagues, leaders, and funding agencies will pay dividends, for the same needs apply here. Not only must you present empirical evidence that supports the change you seek, but you also have to become adept at understanding the differing needs and priorities of others in the organization. The same persuasive tactics will not work for everyone. You will need to be skilled at recognizing each leader's role in the larger organization and providing them the evidence that helps them understand how your initiatives fit within the areas they oversee. The best change management may start with the why—and you certainly will need to help them feel the humanism that guides such change—but you also must marshal the evidence that supports that why and moves them to what and how. You need to have a change plan to support implementation.

We also cannot overlook the importance of assembling a team with the proper skill sets and then creating a supportive environment where team members can act on the same qualities you have learned to demonstrate as their leader. Among the experts you will need are those with previous change management experience alongside those with project management expertise. You will need gifted educators who possess passion, enthusiasm, and dedication to this work, as well as an entire staff who are truly lifelong learners themselves. Those who come from public health backgrounds will prove vital assets, as will those with human resource expertise and those with strategic agility. Employees experienced in analytical and data research are important. All will need effective communication skills. Additionally, there's a reality you need to be prepared to encounter—not everyone is cut out for the demands change requires or shows a willingness to learn its necessary skill sets. While obviously, you want to seek out the strengths in all those in your employ, you must be prepared to make difficult decisions and "liberate" those who are not up to the challenge. Failure to take action when action is needed can potentially create a toxic work environment that makes the demanding task of change management more challenging. Identifying likely areas of resistance in advance can go a long way to mitigating the challenges and ensuring successful change implementation.

ACTING ON CHANGE MANAGEMENT PRINCIPLES

The work required of the team you assemble will have change-management needs threaded through everything they do. You're not going to accomplish sustainable change unless you focus on components of change management, which also means that you will be wise to consult with change management experts and bring them into your organization or seek out internal experts. Every institution is different and filled with employees from distinct backgrounds and differing professional experiences, so after working with consultants, you will have to determine how much of the language of formalized change management you will want to adopt, but all will need to understand its central concepts. Whether or not you begin to reference participants as "authorizing sponsors" and "reinforcing sponsors," "current states," and "future states," you will have to develop a structured and strategic multipronged, phased approach to culture change if you are to succeed. Harvard Business School professor Dr. John Kotter has outlined an eight-step model for successful change efforts (see graphic on next page). Steps 1 through 4 help unfreeze the status quo, Steps 5 through 7 introduce new practices, and Step 8 grounds the changes in a new culture to ensure sustainability. Because we know that implementing and sustaining change is difficult, it requires a comprehensive strategy.

It's a goal without a finish line. Half of the goal, from a provider point of view, is to make sure that we have the access to the same type of care in every community, irrespective of the circumstance.

—MICHAEL DOWLING,
President and CEO, Northwell Health

1 — Create urgency

CREATING THE CLIMATE FOR CHANGE

2 — Form a powerful coalition

3 — Create a vision for change

4 — Communicate the vision

ENGAGING & ENABLING THE ORGANIZATION

5 — Empower action

6 — Create quick wins

IMPLEMENTING & SUSTAINING FOR CHANGE

7 — Build on the change

8 — Make it stick

In navigating change, you must know going in that you absolutely will encounter resistance. You not only need to anticipate and be proactive about facing it, but you also must understand what gives rise to it. Part of resistance is universal—humans generally don't like change. They tend to have short-term memories, so you will need to provide consistency rather than a "flavor of the month" approach to how you communicate about the nature of change.

In the diversity and inclusion space, while much of resistance comes from ignorance, a good deal of that ignorance goes beyond unfamiliarity to unspoken or unacknowledged bias and sometimes to overt prejudice. Much of racism, sexism, and ageism, like homophobia and transphobia, is systemic, with tentacles reaching deep within history and entangled within cultural institutions. Creating change when encountering such ancient conventions, particularly when they have so long been closeted from open discussion or acknowledgment, takes relentless pursuit and commitment. Change won't be fast, for the forces that have shaped the need for it are centuries in the making. Few people actively want to be racists or misogynists, but all of us are joined by living inside a larger culture where racism and misogyny have not been addressed and where long-standing organizational structures support both. As a result, your levers should also include a plan to mitigate resistance, for which you have developed a proactive effort to address concerns and build support early in the project.

One tool we have used at Northwell Health to combat resistance generally and reluctance to accept inclusion particularly has been a simple and universal one—storytelling. Sharing stories is central to how we reignite the human connection. They humanize complex experiences and create room for empathy. By encouraging people to share stories both about the difficulties in creating change and the pain that can be caused when people are excluded or dismissed and about the triumphs of successful culture change within an organization, they become engaged and empowered.

At Northwell Health, we share stories informally by using patient and staff stories in meetings and presentations and formally by including experiences in our annual reports, newsletters, blogs, in-house correspondence and outreach through the media. We have made a number of videos that tell the stories of people's lives and experiences and shared these widely. We have collaborated on documentaries that tell of successful systemic change in creating partnerships with patients. While it may feel obvious that sharing stories can generate empathy—a much-needed commodity to create advocates for inclusion—stories are also powerful at creating a sense of urgency, another element required to accomplish change. People must feel that this change must happen, and it needs to happen *now*. That's something good data struggles to accomplish. Data and empirical evidence matter when you are trying to accomplish transformative change, but we should never neglect the power of storytelling to help cement the need.

You will be amazed at the power to connect people through sharing stories. While the journey of change management is a long one, allowing people to share their stories can create identifiable sparks of momentum. You'll see people's enthusiasm at feeling heard and understood or hear their renewed commitment when they participate in storytelling that reveals the truths of their patients' lives. Storytelling alone won't communicate the entirety of a change vision, but it's a backbone element of doing so. In the stories you tell, like all the endeavors you undertake to make change a sustainable reality, you absolutely must adhere to the other principles we have discussed about inclusion, particularly in developing a culture of trust. Only when those you ask to commit to change believe that they can trust you and your team members will they become the agents of change you need. Ultimately, the why you have found is what incentivizes people to trust you and your message. From trust, they begin to form a common core of values and beliefs—precisely what is required for substantive and lasting change.

BUILDING A FRAMEWORK FOR DIVERSITY, INCLUSION, AND HEALTH EQUITY

Part II details each of the foundational pillars of our strategic framework: leadership commitment, education and development, language access, community partnerships, supplier diversity, and workforce.

CHAPTER FIVE

LEADERSHIP COMMITMENT

Good leadership requires you to surround yourself with people of diverse perspectives who can disagree with you without fear of retaliation.

—DORIS KEARNS GOODWIN

Any institution is only as good and as visionary as its leaders. To be successful in creating a diverse and inclusive health organization, you will need to learn how to help your organization's leadership team understand the central importance of this work, for you need them to become champions for this cause. Leaders who guide diversity and inclusion initiatives must have a seat at the senior leadership table and must become adept atarticulating their "why" among those who possess the power to push the organization toward change. The first of many partnership relationships that this book will focus on is the one between you, your fellow leaders, and your mission. Every aspect of the framework we will outline in this book is dependent upon commitment from leaders that is revealed in the American Hospital Association's Equity Campaign to Eliminate Health Care Disparities to make a diverse culture of inclusion a reality.

If you were to walk the hallways of North Shore University Hospital or Long Island Jewish Medical Center, the two original hospitals in the larger Northwell Health system, and found yourself near either of their boardrooms, you'd encounter lots of framed portraits of former board members and physicians who had risen through the ranks to leadership positions. Nearly all would be portraits of White men. This will not come as much of a surprise. You'd find similar portraits in any major US hospital, any corporation, or any institution for that matter. It's simply, if sadly, a measure of the larger history of the United States, where despite being formed from a mosaic of people with origins in every part of the globe, its diversity has been slow to translate into representation in seats of power. This is no condemnation of the people featured in such portraits, for many were pivotal in improving people's lives through their commitment to the importance of healthcare, and some were champions for diversity. But we would be naive to believe that the vision such men brought to the institutions they helped form adequately represented all in the communities they served.

The lack of true partnerships with community residents from places like Spinney Hill by the two hospitals its residents could often see from their front doorsteps continued well into this century. Indeed, until the Northwell Health's team actively started asking patients and community members how they could better serve them, too often any outreach into the neighborhood tended to be of the one-day off-site screening-clinic variety, leading to a belief by its residents that the local hospitals held no real commitment to bettering their long-term health.

The men in most of those portraits probably could not imagine the diversity among the faces that are beginning to join them, for the makeup of those portraits is slowly changing. It has to if we are ever to attain health equity such that the residents of this area have access to the same quality of care as those of Old Westbury, one of the fabled Gold Coast neighborhoods just miles away. Indeed, it is through the expansion and inclusion of diverse leadership portraits that we find a critical first step on the pathway toward equity, as we will discuss in a chapter on workforce later in the book.

COMMITMENT AT THE HIGHEST LEVELS OF LEADERSHIP

The commitment demonstrated by our CEO when he signed the American Hospital Association's Equity of Care Pledge Campaign to Eliminate Health Care Disparities was visionary in 2017. Five years into our journey at the time, we were already well on our way to achieving the standards of the Health Equity Pledge initiative:

1. Increase the accurate collection, stratification and use of race, ethnicity, language preference and other sociodemographic data and use data to identify and solve for health disparities while linking quality to equity in care.

2. Increase cultural competency training to ensure culturally responsive care.

3. Advance diversity in leadership and governance to reflect the communities served.

4. Improve and strengthen community partnerships.[41]

5. Address racism as a public health crisis.

Leadership support for these four tenets of the campaign, like the principles we focus on throughout this book, must be tangible, action oriented, and sustained. And financial support has to follow. That support has to be deeply embedded at the C-suite level and then flow through the whole of the organization. As much as you need the active involvement of CEOs, CFOs, COOs, and others, you must develop a purposeful leadership structure at the site level as well, and the interchange of ideas and data has to flow in both directions.

At Northwell Health, as we've discussed, we not only had a visionary leader in Michael Dowling, one who had long experience in community health policy, but we also had a mandate with the founding of the Zucker School of Medicine and its new curriculum. Our involvement started at the outset. Our coauthor, Dr. Mieres, had worked for what was then the North Shore-LIJ Health System many years before as the director of nuclear cardiology. She was a known entity, respected by the hospital board and by CEO Dowling and highly regarded for the work she had done both as a physician and as a documentarian and author on the cause of creating equality for women in the treatment and prevention of heart disease.

The need for a formalized strategy to diversity within the health system was a conversation Mr. Dowling and Dr. Mieres had shared before, so when he initiated the formation of an office dedicated to diversity and inclusion, he recruited her to return to the health system to lead. Dowling's selection of Dr. Mieres as Northwell Health's first chief diversity and inclusion officer was made because he recognized her unique skill set as a leader, but it should not be omitted that the acceptance of her by others in the health system was aided by the fact that she is a physician, a fact that continues to carry cachet in medical communities and can create authority and engagement as a result. Dr. Mieres and colleague Terri Ann Parnell, RN, DNP, a nurse educator and expert on health literacy, established the Office of Diversity, Inclusion, and Health Literacy. They both understood and appreciated the importance of leadership and set about educating themselves on the best practices of leadership. Moreover, there is important but simple resonance when holding conversations about the importance of diversity in healthcare and medical settings to note that Dr. Mieres is a Black female physician who came to the United States from Trinidad for her higher education. Having a chief diversity and inclusion officer who has shared experiences similar to those of the patients for whom she is the lead advocate can offer the reassurance of understanding and representation. It is also critical to note that the chief diversity and inclusion officer holds a C-level position, something that is vital to ensuring that diversity and inclusion issues are on the agenda at the senior management level. It is imperative that any organization wishing to develop its own leadership model for diversity and inclusion representation follow suit.

MECHANISMS FOR SHARING A MESSAGE AND BUILDING TRUST

With the formation of a new office focused on diversity, inclusion, and health literacy, we were in uncharted waters. There were few best practices in place and few models to draw on, so much of what we saw as necessary design for activating the support of leaders throughout the organization was of our own making. Because we came from medical and academic backgrounds, we were already immersed in a world where we were accustomed to approaching new terrain from a scientific method approach, and we placed a premium on developing evidence-based data. We would never dream of entering a meeting with a C-suite executive without being able to supply evidence that what we were proposing was backed with solid research and data. This provided us important credibility and is a consideration any organization should make as they develop systems customized for their environment. This is particularly critical since the operations undertaken to advance diversity and inclusion do not generate revenue. When you are advancing into new terrain, your mandate requires significant financial and human resources, and you don't directly produce income, you'd better have documentable support on your side to justify why your mission is critical to the larger institution (which in the case of our approach to diversity and inclusion, results in significant cost savings in clinical care and elsewhere and makes Northwell Health a very desirable workplace that can recruit superior talent).

Central to marshaling your arguments, you must understand the interests of all the stakeholders required to support your work. You can, for example, readily convince CEOs and CFOs that despite not producing revenue, these programs generate substantial competitive advantage. Of course, twenty-first-century healthcare, particularly given the ready access consumers have to information and their ability to compare healthcare providers, is an extremely competitive industry. While we passionately believe there is value in returning to aspects of older physician/patient approaches that reflect a humanistic-minded healthcare model prioritizing the ability to know their patients as individuals and meet them on their home ground (sometimes quite literally), long gone are the days when patients have no choice in who they turn to for their care. If people turn to competitors who make them feel more welcomed or understood and provide them a greater sense of empowerment, when we lose them as patients, obviously, we also lose their revenue. Moreover, we lose status in the larger community. In an age of social media, the ability and frequency of sharing experiences are amplified. People are as apt to rate their neighborhood hospital as they are their neighborhood bistro. Many a hospital has succumbed to not understanding its community and its patient base, and there will always be another entity that will recognize the need in the space they have vacated.

We also work in an era with external incentives to be strategic in the development of diversity and inclusion programs. There now exist mandates under the Affordable Care Act (ACA) that govern many of our functions. For example, the ACA requires providers to offer interpreting and translation services to limited English proficient (LEP) patients free of charge; it also mandates that bilingual staff pass a fluency assessment (the precise details of this ACA requirement, amended in 2020, can be found in Section 92.101 of "Nondiscrimination in Health and Health Education Programs or Activities, Delegation of Authority," a rule by the Centers for Medicare & Medicaid Services).[42] Consider, for a moment, the complexity affiliated with this one requirement: compliance with the ACA means getting fluency accreditation notices into employee files and within databases so that their expertise can be put to work rapidly as needed. As with all such programs where sizable investments in time, training, and people are required, whether in response to a mandate or your own initiative, success in any diversity and inclusion endeavor is impossible without leadership commitment to strategic planning.

In our case, because we had the kind of leadership support that recognized the need to align regulatory requirements, business needs, and quality-of-care benchmarks, we had a leg up. We were blessed with leaders who drove diversity initiatives and were vocal in support of their importance. As we reached to build allyship within the larger organization, much of our job was twofold: (1) to demonstrate that we could positively link the initiatives we were undertaking to the improvement of patient outcomes, and (2) to develop, improve, and build trust in the communities we serve and establish relationships with our community members so that the health system is seen as a valued partner. We needed to become the place they *chose* to turn to for their care, to become the place they were proud to have at the heart of their community. It's a tall ask, but ideally, places like hospitals that stand as icons of larger health organizations should feel as familiar and as central to community members as their places of worship and their schools.

As we began developing the structures underneath each of the pillars we identified as crucial to improved health equity, we not only shared those findings with our leadership team, but we also began to publish those findings and present them at conferences among peers all over the world. The interest and engagement we found as we presented data solidified leadership belief in the importance of the work we were doing and secured additional investment in it.

In addition to presenting the evidence we accumulated, we shared the stories we encountered. While the data we produce is key in contextualizing the work we do, we can never lose sight of the ways we touch individual human lives. It is vital that we remind leadership this is the case and share stories with them as well. We've also discovered that you have to create archives of your actions and decisions. And of your stories. You have to document your success and your failures. Your policies have to be written and brought to the attention of others. We operate under the mantra, "If it isn't written down, it doesn't exist." And then you've got to follow up every document with in-person contact so that there is a face behind the policy.

All of this work created interest in what we were doing. It was a way to say constantly, "This work matters." To be successful in the development of the work we do requires constant outreach into every department and division of the healthcare system and into every niche of the community. When the center was in its fledgling stages, as we tried to bring our existence to the awareness of other offices and departments, we had to beg people to take meetings with us, bribing them with doughnuts and coffee or pizza lunches. The most common response to a request to meet with another entity in our larger organization was typically, "Now what office are you with again?" We had to be relentless.

Over time, interest became entropy. When DiversityInc, the leading diversity-focused publication for corporate affairs in the United States, first launched their health top ten healthcare system rankings, Michael Dowling brought their list to an executive council meeting. He challenged us, saying, "We need to be on this." We immediately made a promise that we would make that list within two years. It's one of those goals we can proudly say we accomplished, and we can now boast that we have been assessed by DiversityInc as the number-one healthcare system in the United States in 2020 and 2021.

THE ROLE OF GOVERNANCE

To accomplish such goals takes sustained leadership commitment. With that commitment in place, you then have to create structures that support communication, information sharing, innovative problem solving, and governance. Creating a multilayered governance structure is an important part of developing a formalized, intentional approach to ensure sustainability.

Creating a multilayered governance structure is an important part of developing a formalized, intentional approach to ensure sustainability.

We started by forming an executive council, officially titled the Executive Council on Diversity, Inclusion, and Health Literacy. By having direct representation with C-suite executives specifically focused on issues of diversity and inclusion, we not only have access at the executive and board level, but we also help create a larger culture that trickles down throughout the organization. The committee is chaired by the president and chief executive officer of Northwell Health and comprises other members of senior leadership, including the chief diversity and inclusion officer. When others see buy-in at the executive level, they recognize the importance the system places on our initiatives. Moreover, the executive council draws on the brainpower and experience of top-level executives to serve as a think tank.

We then furthered our leadership governance structure by developing numerous additional councils, each representing various stakeholders and all structured under the executive council so that they can be certain their concerns can be heard at the highest levels. They include the following, among others:

- Physician Council on Diversity and Health Equity: This council represents the specific needs of the physician community, including the diverse needs of our residents and fellows. The council was established in an effort to promote institutional excellence in patient care, patient health outcomes, and research by linking quality to equitable healthcare delivery. Comprised of senior-level full-time faculty members from the volunteer staff society and recommended service lines, the council is cochaired by the chief medical officer, deputy chief medical officer, and the academic chair of the Department of Medicine.

- Advanced Clinical Practice Council: Focuses on nurses, nurse practitioners, and physician assistants.

- Diversity and Inclusion Workforce Council: Focuses on establishing and maintaining workforce diversity by fostering a culture of inclusion where every team member can be their authentic self in the workplace.

- System Effective Communication Committee: Focuses on patient education and language and communication-access services.

- Supplier Diversity Council: Oversees strategies for how to create and foster economic opportunity in the communities we serve by creating partnerships with minority, women, LGBTQIA+, veterans, and people-with-disabilities-owned vendors and partners.

- LGBTQIA+ Patient Care Education Task Force: Founded to implement and evaluate a system-wide educational curriculum to build awareness around the unique needs and challenges facing the LGBTQIA+ (lesbian, gay, bisexual, transgender, queer or questioning, intersex, and asexual or allied) patient populations.

- System Site Council on Diversity and Health Equity: Focuses on grassroots building, taking from the top down and deploying strategies and initiatives throughout the organization. The site council identifies issues connected to the needs of the local community and implements initiatives that showcase best practices capable of being scaled at the larger organizational level.

- Committee on Community Health: A subcommittee of the board of trustees focusing on ensuring the alignment of Northwell Health's community and population health strategy with the community health needs assessments of the various communities served.

All committees and councils that assist the Northwell Health's Center for Equity of Care are critical to gathering the perspectives of the constituents they represent, and all are able to communicate and coordinate with both the leadership of the center and with the executive council. Each council operates under specific charters that govern their makeup and the scope of their responsibilities. We have worked hard to develop a governance structure where virtually all stakeholders in the Northwell Health system have access to representation on diversity and inclusion concerns in the full knowledge that they will be heard by leadership. Moreover, this governance structure provides additional ways to communicate about and gain feedback on policies and initiatives developed by our office. These various councils work in a manner parallel to numerous Business Employee Resource Groups (BERGs) that have formed throughout the system, all aligned with the goal of committing to high-quality patient care and community wellness by engaging employees; enhancing talent recruitment, retention, and development; and serving as ambassadors to internal/external communities.

LEADERSHIP MODELS

We have worked tirelessly to match our words with actions as we develop the leadership structure required to guide change. That also means being intentional in how we cultivate leadership within our office that is reflective of the values of humanism. This is a driving force in our recruitment of talent as well, for we have developed a collaborative leadership team and workforce that is solution minded. We try to be mindful of the cultural nuances that exist within an organization that has as many employees as a small city and focus energy on figuring out how to navigate them. We recognize that in order to accomplish our mission, we must develop trusting and openly communicative relationships with all of our stakeholders in an awareness that each has a unique perspective and distinct needs. In a health system as large as ours, there are literally dozens and dozens of different departments and divisions, each with their own mandates, but one of the constant reminders we offer is that the benefits of diversity and inclusion cut across all interests. We have to live by the principles of humanism, and that means fostering genuine relationships in every facet of the system. When we establish trust, then people are going to act as advocates and champions and sponsors of this effort. To accomplish trust means understanding the psychology of the leaders in each division of the larger organization and learning to understand the difficulties they face and the nature of their institutional roles. Success in change management means developing

When we establish trust, then people are going to act as advocates and champions and sponsors of this effort.

a choreography that fits the dance of the organization, which requires experience and reflection, as well as authenticity. And that all starts by having grounded leaders.

A grounded leader is skilled in selecting the right team, for it really does take the aligned, coordinated effort of an entire team to advance the principles of diversity and inclusion. They have to represent a diversity of experience and perspectives reflective of those goals as well. That is why we have filled positions with excellent candidates from within other divisions of Northwell Health who demonstrate a passion for helping achieve the goals of the center, and we have been open to recruiting people from outside the system who offer a variety of frontline, research, and leadership experiences. Selecting the right team is largely about celebrating the diversity of backgrounds while aligning with a collective philosophy. In order to develop teams that are creative, communicative, and willing to stimulate original ideas while rallying means you have to recognize that education and career development must be continuous. The leaders of such teams also need opportunities to continue their education and refine their leadership styles. We cultivate an office environment built on the belief that we are all learning every day. As a result, we operate in a spirit of mentoring and reverse mentoring and recognizing everyone in the center has experiences to share and lessons they have learned that deserve to be passed on. We require all new leaders on the Center for Equity of Care team are provided at least two years of mentoring. We hold the view that one has to learn to be a leader in a manner parallel to how each of us had to go about systematically studying in our fields of professional and academic expertise.

At Northwell Health, we benefited initially from having visionary leaders who recognized such needs and who made change a priority. Recognizing how vital such leadership was, with the formation of the Center for Equity of Care, we set about professionalizing our own leadership training and then building relationships throughout the system. Doing so was foundational to realizing each of the other pillars we identified as required to succeed on our mission.

WHAT ARE THE NEXT STEPS ON YOUR JOURNEY TOWARD HEALTH EQUITY?

- Use the power of storytelling, and share a story from within your organization that either illustrates the support you already have in place from a senior leader or one that demonstrates why the need for such support is evident.

- Is the driving force to address diversity and inclusion in your organization a mandate from your senior leadership, which now needs to infiltrate the whole culture? Or is it a grassroots vision that needs to elevate the organization by recruiting senior managers to its cause?

- If the former, how can you place senior leaders in visible positions on diversity and inclusion opportunities that can demonstrate their commitment to the rest of the organization?

- If the latter, what aspects of humanism are central to individual leader's beliefs and experiences that you can draw on to engage them? Who are your best targets for cultivating leadership alliances? What appeals to your leaders regarding this work?

- What motivates your leaders to want to commit to this important work?

- Have you curated internal data and external research that helps you demonstrate both the need and the benefit from an organizational perspective and embrace diversity and inclusion? Where and with whom have you shared these materials? With whom do you share your insights, perspectives, trends, and analysis?

- What would you identify as the three most central attributes of your organization's core culture? Where do those attributes pose challenges for implementing your initiatives? Where do they present opportunities or suggest effective strategies for managing change? How do these attributes align with your vision for change?

CHAPTER SIX

EDUCATION AND DEVELOPMENT

Ignorance causes exclusion.
Education enables inclusion if you do it right.

—KATHY GALLO, RN, PHD
Chief Learning Officer and Founding Dean of the
Graduate School of Nursing at Hofstra/Northwell

According to the American Medical Association, poor health literacy is a stronger predictor of a person's health than age, income, employment status, education level, and race. Deficits in health literacy are linked to a higher risk of death and more emergency room visits and hospitalizations. People with poor literacy are more likely to have a chronic disease and less likely to get the healthcare they need.[43] Patients with poor health literacy create a revolving door effect where we treat and discharge only to have them appear in our clinics and emergency rooms again. The means to stop the door from revolving is education. Educating patients is tricky and ongoing. You can't do it if you don't first make patients see themselves as active agents—partners—in their own care. And you can't do it if you are not constantly educating your workforce in ways that ensure they act on their strongest impulses to connect with and treat people with consistent dignity and respect, making them feel welcome, heard, and valued.

There are any number of characteristics that make us human. Many, of course, are found in the Hippocratic Oath many of you swore to uphold, including some version of this one: "I will remember that I remain a member of society, with special obligations to all my fellow human beings, those sound of mind and body as well as the infirm." Here are just a few additional traits, some that also echo the oath we view as essential for those of us working in healthcare if we are to successfully create human connections:

- a capacity not to be judgmental and accept people for who they are and respect their beliefs and customs

- a will to remember that there is an art to medicine as well as science and that warmth, sympathy, and understanding may outweigh the surgeon's knife or the chemist's drug

- an ability to admit when we're wrong

- a willingness to actively listen

- a lifelong desire to learn and grow

- a determination to understand a patient's needs and recognize that they are more than a composite of their symptoms

- an ability to effectively communicate with honesty and clarity

If we fail any of these traits, we will never accomplish the task of creating health equity for all. Those of us who serve patients in capacities other than as medical doctors may not formally swear the oath, but we should hold ourselves as bound to its equivalent.

The last three traits on our list cannot be overstated. We participate in professions that are fluid and where knowledge is always growing; we must grow with it. How we apply the knowledge we attain must recognize that we treat patients, not diseases. Gifted clinicians, applying every tool at their disposal and employing those tools from a wealth of current knowledge, cannot sustain a patient's health status if they fail to communicate with the patient. That communication has to be honest and clear, and it must extend an imperative for patients to become active partners in their own care.

Take one of the most common interactions in the provider/patient partnership as a revealing example: patient adherence to medication use. As the former US surgeon general C. Everett Koop so aptly stated, "Drugs don't work in patients who don't take them." Medication adherence can roughly be defined as when a patient takes their medications according to the prescribed dosage, time, frequency, and direction. There may well be many reasons a patient is not adherent, many of them directly connected to the social determinants of health, including difficulty affording a medication or a lack of health literacy to understand its usage or importance. But whatever might create nonadherence, one omnipresent factor is a breakdown in effective communication between the patient and their provider about the vital role the medication holds in their life.

Consider this common patient example as told by Dr. Marie Brown, an internist and assistant professor at Rush University Medical Center in Chicago:

> Mrs. [S.], a new patient to my practice, told me on her first visit that she was taking three drugs for Type 2 diabetes. She was an obese forty-year-old with a recent A1C of 10. While in the waiting room, she listed her medications: insulin, metformin, and a sulfonylurea. In the exam room, the medical assistant reviewed the patient's medications, including frequency and dosing. Because the patient's drug regimen was apparently not working, I faced adding a fourth drug or increasing her insulin, which would most likely also increase her weight.
>
> I had just read an article on medication nonadherence, so instead of escalating therapy I paused and asked if she actually took her medications.
>
> "Yes," she replied.
>
> "Do you take them every day?" I asked.
>
> She said yes again and denied that there were days when she would skip.
>
> I wondered what I was missing.
>
> "When was the last time you took your medicine?" I asked.
>
> She replied, "Three months ago." Aha!

When I asked her why, she said her insurance had changed and she didn't have a doctor. So, in her mind, she took her medicine every day—when she had it.[44]

Dr. Brown's story conveys a great deal about medication adherence and even more about effective patient communication. Not only does her interaction with her patient reveal some important best practices about asking the right questions and really listening to patient answers, but it also demonstrates that we have to treat the *whole* patient, which necessarily includes their insurance status, their literacy on their health conditions, and their perception of their own role in achieving a healthy status.

To further illustrate the needs of holistic health and the interactions of the social determinants of health as they also apply to patient diversity, let us share a patient example from our own experience.

This story offers an intriguing but not uncommon twist to the difficulties underlying effective communication. After successfully intervening and saving JR's life when he suffered a heart attack, a Northwell Health cardiologist placed him on a beta-blocker as a long-term prevention measure to ward off heart failure. She had observed that JR appeared to understand English, so she interacted with him in English as she explained the benefits of the medication she had prescribed and the importance of following its dosage requirements. JR seemed engaged when his doctor discussed the medication and other actions he needed to take in his cardiac care. Yet months later, JR returned to the hospital with symptoms of worsening heart disease and said that he'd stopped taking his prescribed medication. He offered no explanation. The doctor deemed him noncompliant. Sometime later, during his consultation appointment, one of the nurses engaged JR in Spanish and learned that he had stopped taking the beta-blocker because he had a wife twenty years his junior, and he feared that the beta-blocker would interfere with his ability to be intimate with her. Trained to treat acute conditions and save lives, his doctor found his reasoning perplexing.

From the scientifically analytical perspective of trying to prolong life and return patients to health, the physician's initial reaction to JR's chosen course of action makes perfect sense. JR's case unnerved his doctor. Once she had time to process what the nurse had told her, the doctor realized she was guilty of having judged JR, not only for placing his desire to be intimate with his young wife ahead of prolonging his life but also for not fully taking into account the potential impact of the age difference in the couple's relationship. Despite his apparent English comprehension, she began to wonder if he had fully understood her explanation of his condition and its treatment. Had she placed the potential side effects of the beta-blocker in their full context? Had JR truly realized that failure to take his medication could lead to his death? Had she, upon learning his reason for stopping his medication, acted on unconscious bias? She feared she had dismissed him as noncompliant rather than learning his story. Had she understood more about his life and his concerns, might she have chosen a different beta-blocker or discussed how vital such medication was to JR's survival in a different manner? And she might have provided all communication through a qualified Spanish inter- preter. She needed for JR to become a coarchitect of his healthy heart plan; she wondered if she had failed to find a method of communication that could form the foundation of such a partnership.

To fully admit our humanity necessarily means facing our indi- vidual frailties and the bias we form from our life experiences. Pride, desire, myopia, prejudice, judgment, arrogance, guilt: These are all traits as ordinary and as omnipresent in human beings as any of those on the list with which we opened this chapter. It's only when we stop to confront such traits that we can grow—as providers and as patients. In the case of JR, his doctor took a step back and confronted the bias

*To fully admit our humanity necessarily means facing
our individual frailties and the bias we form
from our life experiences.*

his case had exposed in herself and looked anew at the role language may have held in restricting his full comprehension.

Her experience confronting what a closer look at JR's case revealed was not substantially different from several cases highlighted in the documentary *Rx: The Quiet Revolution*. Examining a "meet the patient where they are at" philosophy through innovative approaches to healthcare in Maine, the Mississippi Delta, San Francisco, and Alaska, the film chronicles health delivery models that apply human connections in order to gain patient trust. The clinicians we meet in the film recognize that if their patients are to become engaged and committed to acting on treatments and therapies necessary to improve their health, their caregivers must come to know them, understand their home environments and communities, and be able to communicate with them in a way that is meaningful to them. In JR's case, his recognition that erectile dysfunction is a common side effect of beta-blockers was personal and meaningful to him, as personal as asking many diabetics patients to quench their desire for high-carbohydrate foods they have loved since childhood, as meaningful as telling a single working parent that they have to improve the quality of their sleep.

By pressing beyond the conditioning of her formal medical training, JR's doctor was rewarded by finding new ways for her patients to become partners in their own care. She realized that she needed to examine what new tools she could use to educate her patients. Altering her approach to patient communication was an important part of her own reignited desire for human connection.

THE FIRST STEPS ON THE JOURNEY

The personal and professional realizations experienced by JR's doctor reflect the experiences those of us in Center for Equity of Care at Northwell Health have had in our own careers and form a reminder about the role education holds in our work. Education has been a central component for all that we do in advocating for diversity and inclusion. You will find the need to effectively educate patients and staff on the issues surrounding health equity reform as key to succeeding with any systematic approach you develop.

It is difficult to educate those who work within any healthcare system without data. Race, ethnicity, and language (REL) data pose enormous difficulties to collect generally, oftentimes because patients refuse to provide such information. Without data coordination across a system, it's extremely difficult to assess your needs. One of the reasons we began the discussion of our pillars with an emphasis on the need for leadership commitment is because addressing healthcare disparities requires the full involvement not only of your entire organization but coordination with other care providers, health plans, and local, state, and federal agencies. This is particularly critical and difficult from a staff and patient education perspective and unachievable without quality leadership.

The Agency for Healthcare Research and Quality of the Department of Health and Human Services lists just some of the challenges we face with REL data collection:

- how to ask patients and enrollees questions about race, ethnicity, and language and communication needs

- how to train staff to elicit this information in a respectful and efficient manner

- how to address the discomfort of registration/admission staff (hospitals and clinics) or call center staff about requesting this information

- how to address potential patient or enrollee pushback respectfully

- how to address system-level issues, such as changes in patient registration screens and data flow[45]

Because these topics are so sensitive and because patient health outcomes are so closely tied to being able to communicate effectively, you have to transform how you ask patients questions as well as how you apply the data you gather. With very few best practices in place, as we contemplated our approach to gathering patient REL data, we started by examining how we might standardize data collection. By engaging with our employees and our community members, particularly through our Business Employee Resource Groups (BERGs), we learned what their concerns were regarding data collection, including their worries about maintaining privacy. Those conversations presented great insight on ways data should be collected and provided us with a roadmap of how to further standardize our race, ethnicity, sexual orientation, and gender identity fields across our data systems.

In something of a chicken-and-egg scenario, we saw immediately that success in improving the data we collected would be accomplished by providing education and training. As we began to meet with our patient registration team, we had them guide us by sharing difficult responses they received from patients who found race and ethnicity questions intrusive. From there, we partnered with their team as we developed our approach to education. Working with the physician leader development program, the patient registration team took the reins in making electronic medical record (EMR) changes so that it was easier for physicians to document new fields in the patient record. Next came direct consultation with physicians and other clinicians. Bringing clinicians on board in redesigning aspects of the EMR helped them understand how such data proved relevant to the ways they interacted with their patients. For example, making certain that patient education and discharge instructions are reviewed with patients in their preferred language directly correlates to fewer return hospital visits, better medication compliance, and better attendance at follow-up appointments. This link between patient data and improved patient outcomes is key for your own strategic plan. Actions that don't improve patient outcomes hold little meaning.

Our journey to eliminate all health disparities is rooted in our commitment to diversity, inclusion and health equity. The solutions are shared via education, and clinical avenues persistently and relentlessly move us forward to our goal to eliminate disparities and provide the very best care for everyone. This focus requires leadership, courage and a moral compass like no other.

—IRA NASH, MD
Professor of Cardiology, Associate Dean for Leadership Development, Zucker School of Medicine; Host, the award-winning "Well Said" podcast and radio broadcast

PROMOTING HEALTH LITERACY

Accomplishing quality outcomes for diverse patients means educating staff in every subdiscipline. This includes training anyone who has a patient-facing role, whether that is in patient records, patient outreach, accounting, or any number of business functions. It also includes training clinicians on best practice methods for communicating with patients and ensuring that they have the opportunity to gain the health literacy required to become their own best advocates.

One primary method we employ with patients is "teach back." We ask that our providers never leave a patient medical encounter without asking the patient to share what they understood in their own words. If a patient understands the information shared with them, they are able to "teach back" effectively. A provider can ask the patient directly to explain what they understood from their conversation about their health, or they can use other questions that provide a measure of their comprehension. For example, a doctor might ask her patient, "Your husband couldn't come with you today. What will you tell him about the changes we made to your medicines today?" This kind of approach acknowledges the patient's dignity while also assessing their understanding.

As with all aspects of inclusion, maintaining the patient's dignity is paramount. We train clinicians in best practices for asking patients questions about their understanding of medical terminology, diagnoses, and treatment plans. In these endeavors, we parallel the approaches taught at the Zucker School of Medicine and at the Hofstra Northwell School of Nursing and Physician Assistant Studies. Among those approaches, we encourage our clinical staff to implement a more humanistic model of health communication other humanistic communication, such as learning and then addressing patients by their preferred name and using models and visual aids to enhance their communication. We teach providers to direct their explanations and comments to the patient rather than to a translator or to family members and pay attention to their own body language and physical proximity to the patient. We recognize that just as people are brought comfort by communicating in a language that is preferable to them, having someone sit next to them, acknowledge them by name, and show a desire to know them and understand them, all to create an environment where frank, clear conversations can take place that better ensure patient understanding. We encourage staff to consider the physical layout of the spaces where they communicate and their position in that space so that they do not loom over a patient restricted to a bed or place a desk between themselves and their patient. We help provide mechanisms for considering clear ways of explaining medical terms and provide suggestions for making procedures and medical devices less imposing by explaining, in simple terms, how they work or what they reveal.

In a similar vein, we try to help educate our team members on how to create documents and discharge instructions, among other written documents, in ways that foster patient comprehension. Creating health-literate documents is no small challenge. Not only is much of medical communication inherently complex, but also we've long worked inside a sector that has seemed intent on obfuscation. Just as we encourage our physicians and other providers to communicate with patients about complex medical terminology by supplementing explanations with visual aids, metaphors, and illustrations—communicating in terms a patient can understand—we look at health materials with the aim of achieving the best possible clarity. Using things like visual guides is important and something we look for when turning to vendors for patient education material or when creating our own. It's important to find clear ways to explain medical jargon and describe medical procedures while defining terms in a health-literate way. Some health organizations try to look at patient metrics such as the highest grade level attained or attempt to identify patients by their professions, or they attempt to assess reading levels and similar perceived measures of literacy. However, after reviewing our experience, we decided to do away with such attempts at assessment. Instead, we employ a universal precautions approach and treat all communication with the assumption that no one has knowledge of its specialized content. That way, we avoid the trap of making assumptions, such as believing that because someone has an advanced degree or works in the medical field that they have attained health literacy about the specifics of their own condition or that they can separate an intellectual understanding from an emotional reaction when conversing about their health. It also helps staff members avoid unconscious bias by making assumptions about health literacy based on factors of physical appearance. Additionally, we provide resources for patients to ask questions that emerge from materials associated with their care, just as we try to create an atmosphere during direct patient encounters for them to engage with their clinician.

WHY EDUCATION MATTERS

The most important outcome of patient/clinician communication is that patients know that they have a partner dedicated to their care. They need to understand their own role and responsibilities in treating their condition. Helping foster that sense of trust creates greater space for more global applications of the National Prevention Strategy.

The most important outcome of patient/clinician communication is that patients know that they have a partner dedicated to their care.

For providers, not only can they realize improved outcomes for their patients through enhancing their education, but there also are important business repercussions as well. As we move away from fee-for-service models and toward value-based care, there is an incentive to block the old revolving door back to the emergency room and frequent hospital readmissions or redundant testing. Twenty-first-century medicine requires us to see that point of care treatment is only a very small part of the full continuum of patient encounters.

If we want our patients to become partners in their care, we have to gain their trust, and we have to communicate with them in ways that don't make them feel belittled. And we have to provide them health education based on facts, facts that empower them. Education and effective communication start with making certain all patients have access to their care while communicating in their preferred language, which is the focus of the next chapter.

WHAT ARE THE NEXT STEPS ON YOUR JOURNEY TOWARD HEALTH EQUITY?

- Share a story from within your organization when an instance of improving a patient's understanding of their condition and treatment plan resulted in them taking an active, responsible role in their own health journey.

- Have you conducted a survey to establish benchmarks for how well you provide health-literate interactions and materials so that your patients'/consumers' interests and experiences are measured? If so, what measure have you put in place to act upon its results?

- What measures do you have in place to really know who your patients are or where they come from?

- What employee educational programs do you have in place to promote health literacy? What patient educational programs do you have in place to promote health literacy?

- Do you have a team in place dedicated to ensuring that all patient-facing documents and materials have been reviewed for health literacy needs?

LANGUAGE ACCESS

If you talk to a man in a language he understands, that goes to his head. If you talk to him in his own language, that goes to his heart.

—NELSON MANDELA

Imagine you are in a foreign country where you do not speak the language. You can't read the signs. You can't understand a single word being uttered by those around you. There are no familiar faces. Now imagine you are injured and trying to ask for help.

It is impossible to communicate effectively with a patient if you don't communicate in a language that they prefer. If we deny this simple truth, we have failed the Hippocratic Oath, we have failed our patients, and we have failed our humanism.

Remember the sad example shared about a COVID-19 patient who died from respiratory failure because he would not leave his oxygen mask in place? Only after his death did the clinicians in an overtaxed emergency room realize that English was not the man's preferred language. It's one of far too many tragic, potentially avoidable deaths in which an inability to communicate with a patient in their preferred language is a significant contributing factor. This example might have you thinking about WR's story from the introduction; WR was the eighteen-year-old Cuban American who is permanently confined to a wheelchair because of a misdiagnosis that hinged on a "Spanglish" misunderstanding of the word *intoxicado*. Sometimes miscommunication can have dire consequences.

Before you can fix such a failure, you have to be aware that it exists. One of the first steps we took was to assess just where Northwell Health already stood. We set about gauging our organizational effectiveness and capacity by participating in a Communication Climate Assessment Tool (CCAT) survey developed by the American Medical Association. We participated in the survey alongside fifty of our peer institutions, and in our case, focused on a snapshot of four of our hospitals. From this survey, we learned a great deal about a number of hard truths that would help us develop our pillars for equity of care, but among them, the one that demonstrated an alarming weakness was "Language Access." Indeed, upon examining the CCAT survey results, we were shocked to discover that Northwell Health's scores for language access were so poor that they literally couldn't be benchmarked against peer organizations. While we fared far better in other important categories, we agreed that if we were unable to communicate effectively with our patients in the languages they found comfortable, we would never be able to address the other pillars. This is a critical point about improving diversity and inclusion in a health organization: no one aspect of the pillars we have identified can be severed from others. For example, we cannot meaningfully address language access without improving cultural competency education, and we'll never achieve patient health literacy without refining both.

We were transparent about the results of the survey and shared them with our executive leadership. Knowing that we worked in an environment with leaders who would look at this survey and not just highlight the areas where we were successful but also take steps necessary to address our deficits says a lot about our organizational culture and its ability to accept challenges. Among those challenges, we discovered there existed few standardized policies or procedures related to topics of diversity and inclusion and no standardized approaches to language access or health literacy education. Moreover, there were no individuals within the organization charged with over-seeing these vital areas. Adding to our challenges, Northwell Health had undergone such rapid growth that we didn't have standardization from one facility to another across a broad spectrum of language access policies. Acquisitions occurred across a number of extraordinarily diverse communities, so the specific needs of patient populations were unique from facility to facility generally and visibly so in language access needs. As we've already underscored, this tremendous expansion was occurring in one of the most linguistically diverse places in the country. Close to 50 percent of Northwell Health patients speak a preferred language other than English. Across the totality of our service area, you might hear 176 different languages spoken on any given day. On one recent day, we had eighty-three patients in the emergency room in *one* hospital who didn't speak English.

Not only did we have this vast unmet need without any standardized linguistic practices in place, but we also were collecting almost no useful language data about our patients. And certainly, we had not examined the problem of language access from a clinical ramification standpoint. We could look into our waiting rooms or walk out into the streets of the neighborhoods where we worked and see the obvious anecdotal evidence that we served a vastly diverse population, yet our data didn't show that to be true because we weren't collecting the relevant data in an accurate, meaningful way. With dozens of facilities, each with its own way of providing services, interpreting regulations, and collecting data, the truth was we didn't really know who our patients were. From a purely statistical point of view, we couldn't know what a big problem we had on our hands because we had no data to indicate there was a problem. Yet our experiences, like that illustrated by JR, whom we met in the last chapter, reminded us daily that not only did we have a problem, but it also was affecting patient outcomes.

The problem of language access is far from one dimensional; you can't simply place a machine or remote interpretation service in a hospital emergency room and solve the problem. Our experiences taught us that even if you provide language access services to individuals in their preferred language, if you're not doing it in a health literate and culturally sensitive way, it will not achieve the desired result. We might be able to interpret what we tell a patient into the language they've heard since they were born, but if they can't comprehend the results or they don't know what dosage of medication they are supposed to take when they return home, the comfort of a familiar language won't be sufficient to improve their outcome. The education needed—for patients and for providers—must incorporate all the components discussed in the previous chapter alongside improved language access if we are to realize the best outcomes. That starts by knowing who a patient is, how they prefer to communicate, and what they understand about their health.

AN APPROACH TO ENHANCING LANGUAGE ACCESS

To accomplish these kinds of changes, you need patient data. Our success in improving patient care has come, in no small part, by changing the kinds of patient data we collect and getting an eclectic variety of stakeholders on board with doing so. We were successful in helping our stakeholders understand that having patient data about their preferred language related directly to their health literacy. The more we understood who our patients are and where they came from through communicating in a language that brings them comfort, the more we could educate them about their health and coarchitect plans to move them toward optimal health.

Accomplishing greater access for limited English proficient (LEP) patients meant new approaches were required. These included such things as creating "i-speak" cards for our deaf and hard of hearing patients, which provide them a means to demonstrate their language access needs and interact with their providers. It meant creating multilanguage information kiosks in high-traffic facilities. It meant what might seem small things, like creating comfortable, attractive entrance areas in our hospitals that welcomed patients with greetings in several languages and that employed art that offered cultural familiarity. Our initiative operated from this belief: the only way to form a partnership with another human is to understand what's meaningful to them and then frame the information you need to communicate in a way that they're going to listen to.

Being able to communicate effectively starts with communicating in a language that encourages patients to feel confident they understand the information shared with them. Then they can engage in decisions affecting their health in the knowledge that they can meet the responsibilities required of them. When patients see their own behaviors have positive influences on their health, they feel empowered. Empowerment starts with engagement.

In order to accomplish engagement when speaking about language access, it is imperative that we understand using a language the patient *understands* is insufficient. We must communicate in the language they *prefer*. For patients who are multilingual or proficient in English, language preference still matters. As many of our patient stories have already illustrated, medical settings are, by nature, stressful places. Often, the patient has arrived at a moment of a health emergency, placing them at a point of vulnerability. They may be receiving a life-altering or life-threatening diagnosis. Not only do they find themselves in a foreign environment experiencing a moment that is riddled with stress, but they are also likely to be in pain or discomfort, and too frequently, they must interact with clinicians they have never met before. If the patient and the medical professionals with whom they are interacting do not share a common language at all, let alone one preferred by the patient, the stressors are only exaggerated.

Empowerment is directly linked to personal identity—how you see yourself. If you typically communicate in a language other than

English and you hear your provider speak only English, what does that do to your sense of identity? There is a power misbalance created by the situation, one further emphasized by the gulf of health literacy between patient and provider. Too often, vulnerable patients are met with what is, to them, incomprehensible jargon. And making matters more stressful, too often, there is no sense of shared identity; patients don't see themselves reflected in their providers' faces. If communication occurs outside your preferred language, the circumstance becomes one of a stranger telling you what to do rather than you taking an active role in your own life and health. People are empowered when they have the knowledge, resources, ability, and motivation to identify and make healthy choices.

From the clinician's viewpoint, how can you present the patient with the tools, resources, education, knowledge, and communication necessary for them to make informed decisions about their care if you are not able to reach them in their preferred language? How do you establish a relationship, one where the ability to trust—in both directions—is imperative? Decision making is a complex process influenced by personal, cultural, social, economic, and environmental factors, including an individual's ability to meet their daily needs. Expanding their knowledge about their condition provides them motivation to have a positive impact on it.

People are empowered when they have the knowledge, resources, ability, and motivation to identify and make healthy choices.

CREATING AN EDUCATIONAL FRAMEWORK

So how do we create a framework that amplifies empowerment through language access? For us, it started with asking a patient's preferred language from the first point of contact, and it meant asking it in those terms: "What is your preferred language to communicate regarding your healthcare?" That approach, as distinct from a question like, "Do you speak English?" should not be underestimated. It is an approach that provides patient choice and empowerment. Not only is this the language of our intake form, but it also is consistent with the training we provide all of our staff when speaking with patients. And once that preferred language is noted, it is added to their electronic medical record (EMR)—prominently appearing in its banner right next to the patient's name and date of birth. This is purposeful, reflecting not only the importance we place on identifying the language of choice for the patient but the centrality of its importance to the clinician.

At Northwell Health, we have also built a real-time, interactive dashboard and linked it to the patient EMR that allows us to see where a patient is coming from, know their preferred language and their diagnosis, and identify whether there are healthcare disparities. Encountering the patient's preferred language the moment a clinician sees their record allows them to make certain that interpreters are present for all direct interactions, and it means that translated vital documents will be presented to the patient throughout the continuum of their care—not just at the hospital or in their physician's office, but at the pharmacy, with the physical therapist, at a lab, clinic, or outreach facility, and in interactions with the business office. And in 2017, we introduced Race, Ethnicity, and Language (REL) Training, a web-based registrar training program for frontline staff and managers to obtain accurate patient race, ethnicity, and preferred language information.

To guarantee that documents shared with patients are translated into their preferred language, we created a vital documents portal through our system intranet. This portal allows providers real-time access to translated versions of essential patient documents, such as consent forms, in over twenty-two languages and braille transcription. The portal ensures that all important documents are presented in the language a patient has chosen and is standardized across all of our facilities and patient touchpoints. Our office oversees the translation of such documents, not just so that they are presented in a patient's preferred language but so that translation occurs in a culturally sensitive and health-literate manner. We oversee all spoken interpretation services as well and hold our interpreter services vendors to the same standard.

Getting the logistics of interpretation right has been part of our ten-year journey. Along the way, we discovered that it was difficult to find vendors that provide health-literate materials generally and certainly not health-literate material in translation. For transcript translation services and often for in-person interpretation services, many vendors rely on artificial intelligence via automated translators. We have tested numerous automated translation services and find that most do a mediocre job at best given the complex, nuanced, and necessarily precise needs of medical translation. Even the best among them is not vetted sufficiently for either medical accuracy or cultural appropriateness. Artificial intelligence certainly cannot replace human interaction and empathy. Most importantly, it is not interactive; you don't get to ask questions of a machine. And machine translation services are notorious for making errors. Consider the implications of these examples of failed translations from popular software (errors often duplicated by those who are untrained and acting in an ad hoc capacity):

- A written document on "fall protection" was titled in Spanish translation as "Otoño Protección." *Otoño* means "autumn" in Spanish.

- "*El constipado*," Spanish for "cold," often is misinterpreted as "constipation."

- The Spanish word for "pregnant"—*embarazada*—is often confused with the English word *embarrassed*.

We saw no meaningful value in such software and went looking for other mechanisms. Where once our gold standard was to have interpretation occur through a two-way communication device with a live interpreter or via a one-way system using third-party software, we've now evolved to using video conferencing with a live interpreter. We initially used dual-phone style devices and had them readily present throughout the health system so that we could meet our goal of having interpretation services to a patient within seconds of a request, but we realized over time that the devices, while very useful, were mechanical, lacked human warmth, and thus were not as patient friendly. With video interpretation services, not only can the patient see the person who is aiding the process by providing interpretation services, quite often, that interpreter can offer a face that looks familiar to the patient or understand relevant aspects of the patient's culture. The familiarity can be comforting and can help build trust with the clinician as well, for the process is purposefully interactive, using a technological interface that encourages the patient to ask questions.

TRAINING QUALIFIED INTERPRETERS

We are enhancing our program further to increase the use of on-site qualified medical interpreters drawn from our staff. "Qualified" is a critical term. A lot of people fall into the belief that because a person speaks a language, they are qualified to interpret for others, which often is labeled as ad hoc interpretation. In many instances, such ad hoc interpreters are used to provide the bulk of language interpretation services. Some were intuitively good at it, but not only is happenstance quality something you cannot count on, but it also neglects the complex knowledge required by skilled interpreters. Medical interpretation is an art form. Professionally trained interpreters become cultural brokers between the patient and their providers, and their responsibilities go far beyond the scope of language. As a result, we don't take a laissez-faire approach to training our employee interpreters. This needs to be true for full-time interpretation staff, trained in-person employee interpreters, and interpreters who work remotely and speak with patients over video or audio devices, whether they are employed by third-party providers or within your health organization.

For our own approach, educating someone on how to be an effective medical interpreter is rigorous and nuanced. Our course requires forty hours of instruction in English, and much of its emphasis explores the ethical issues encountered with medical interpretation. Moreover, when employees train to become interpreters, they have to prove that they are able to interpret while simultaneously fulfilling their role of supplying clinical care or the other responsibilities of their position. Training existing staff represents the gold standard of language interpretation services. It is exceedingly demanding, but to have a live human present who shares the patient's language, is more likely to live in the patient's community, and has a high degree of health literacy creates an invaluable partnership. This not only provides the patient comfort and trust during the medical encounter, but those feelings also follow them out into their interactions in the larger community and cement a belief that their health organization recognizes its community members and wishes to serve their interests.

The near future standard for us will come from mobilizing the diversity of our employee population. Because we live in such a diverse place and because we have over seventy-six thousand employees, we're moving toward training more and more employees to become qualified medical interpreters. An important, systematic literature review survey concluded that the use of professional interpreters was associated with improved clinical care more than was the use of ad hoc interpreters; conclusions from this survey found that professional interpreters "appear to raise the quality of clinical care for LEP patients to approach or equal that for patients without language barriers."[46] When our employees don't just share a language with the patients that they serve but regard them as fellow community members, real relationships develop and through the trust that is established in those relationships, patients become more engaged partners in their care.

Training a sufficient number of qualified bilingual medical interpreters may not be realistic for all health organizations, and even for those who have the capacity to do so, it takes time. Best practices for language interpretation consistently maximize the human contact for patients. For example, even if language interpreters are remote, having a qualified interpreter present through a video device is far superior to a machine translator, even if equipped with state-of-the-art artificially intelligent software. The ability to provide culturally sensitive language translation cannot be met by a machine, nor can it be replicated haphazardly by nonqualified volunteer translators, whether they are a patient's family members or clinical staff. Additionally, as we addressed in the previous chapter, certifying employees as interpreters isn't a linguistic concern alone; translating effectively requires cultural competency and health literacy.

BEYOND QUALIFIED INTERPRETERS

Of course, point of care encounters only represent a small fragment of language access needs, as we realize that communication in the patient's preferred language really is just an entry point to larger health literacy. We have to address numerous other communication materials to help patients attain their best health.

In the written sphere, like the first example, most mass-produced or commercially available health documents not only possess errors, but they also are simply hard to understand. As a result, we've done a lot of work internally to establish guidelines to make sure that materials are health literate and translated in the appropriate manner and written with our diverse population in mind. Most of our materials have been written in house, working closely in partnership with those on our service line representing different specialties. While it certainly takes a clinician with a unique communications skillset to write materials that are distributed to patients or are utilized in our teaching materials with staff education, there's no substitute. We work hard to identify those who have a strong understanding of health literacy, strong writing abilities, and that rare ability to explain complex material in clear, accessible ways.

The Center for Equity of Care collaborates on the production of such materials and then edits them in accordance with rigid specifications. And while it can sound like our approach to editing is on the edge of obsessive, we believe consistency is critical to ensure that the same standards apply all over our system and that patients are met with a unified approach to communication. As a result, we review select documents, right down to the spacing of margins and the size of the font. For us, creating such precise uniformity goes hand in hand with truly reading every document from a patient viewpoint focused on health literacy. We go out of our way to place ourselves in the patient's shoes and rigorously test documents before release. Such attention is a way to ensure readability and clarity. Ensuring uniformity has critical implications of getting the broader reasoning behind health-literate documents to become deeply integrated into the fabric of our Northwell Health culture. The following documents show how we've adjusted our documentation to improve communication for patients.

To our Patient,

Welcome to 9 Tower!

We are happy to have you as our patient. We care about your safety. To help keep you safe, we will be checking on you often, at least once an hour during the day and every two hours at night. This is called 'Rounding'. In addition, we will ask you to remember the following:

1. **Call for help.** If you need help to get out of bed, then please do not try to without calling us. Your call bells should always be nearby. We are here to help you with anything you need.

2. **Use your equipment.** If you require a walker, a cane, crutches, or a brace, please use them. If you are receiving IV fluid that is attached to an IV pole and need us to push it for you, please ask us for help. Also if you need a robe we would be happy to provide you with one..

3. **Maintain proper footwear.** Please do not walk around barefoot. We will be glad to provide you with non-skid socks that you can wear around our unit.

4. **If you are feeling dizzy or not well, stop and let us know!** We want to know how you are feeling.

5. **Always know where your call bell is.** The red button on the remote control is your main call bell. There is also a call bell button on the side rail of your bed. When you are in the bathroom, there is a string to the side that you can pull to tell us that you need help.

6. **Let us light the way.** We want you to be able to see when you are walking around.

7. **If you have any questions, please ask a member of your care team.** When in doubt, ask!

We are happy to help you in any way we can to make your experience with us as safe as possible. Let us know if there is anything more we can do for you.

Before

Your Safety is Very Important to Us!

The information provided below will help you know what you can
do to prevent falls and stay safe while you are in the hospital.

**We will be checking on you at least once every hour during the day
and every two hours at night.**

Always Know Where Your Call Bell Is!	• The red button on your remote control is your <u>call bell.</u> • There is a picture of a nurse on the inside of both side rails of your bed. • If you press this picture it will ring the <u>call bell.</u> • In the bathroom, there is a string on the side of the toilet bowl that you can pull if you need help.
Call for Help!	• <u>Always</u> keep your call bell near you.
Use Your Walking Aids and Equipment!	• Use your walker, cane, crutches or brace if you were told to do so. • If you are on intravenous (IV) fluids attached to a pole or any other equipment with tubing or wires, ask a member of your care team for help when you want to walk.
Wear Proper Footwear!	• Do not walk barefoot. • Non-skid socks are available if needed. • Ask a member of your care team.
Tell Your Care Team How You Are Feeling!	• Tell a member of your care team if you are not feeling well or are feeling dizzy.

If you have any other questions,
please ask a member of your care team!

June 2013

After

We have created rigid internal standards for language access.
You will need to find approaches that fit your system's needs, but of
course, you have no choice but to alter your approach to language
access services not only because ethics demand it but because it is the

law. Federal law requires linguistic services for patients with limited English proficiency (LEP). Title VI of the US Civil Rights Act states that people cannot be discriminated against as a result of their national origin, race, or color, which has been extrapolated to include primary language by the US Office for Civil Rights and Department of Health and Human Services. In addition, healthcare organizations that receive federal funds must provide services in a language that a patient with LEP can understand. The Joint Commission, the main hospital accreditation body in the United States, requires that hospitals collect and record patients' preferred languages for discussing healthcare and have included in their standards the use of qualified medical interpreters for patients whose preferred language is not English.[47]

The results of applying these principles are significant. When people see that the medical professionals to whom they turn actively engage them in their preferred language, not only is their understanding of their healthcare needs improved, but their interest in taking part in things like prevention screenings and follow-up care also is increased, which can create very real improved outcomes like staving off second heart attacks or taking greater responsibility in diabetes management.

If still you hold any doubts about how valuable language access is for achieving quality outcomes, recall the scenario we opened the chapter with: you are traveling in a foreign country, unable to speak the language, and you are injured. Now take it one step further: your injury requires surgical intervention, and your would-be surgeon speaks no English. What's your emotional state as you are about to be placed under anesthesia? Are those emotions you ever want one of your patients to experience while in your care?

WHAT ARE THE NEXT STEPS ON YOUR JOURNEY TOWARD HEALTH EQUITY?

- Share a story from within your organization when a failure to provide communication in a patient's preferred language held important repercussions for the patient's health outcome.

- Have you conducted a survey to establish benchmarks to gauge patient perspectives on the effectiveness of your language access services? Do you have data that reveals what languages are spoken by the patients you serve and for the dominant languages present in your service area?

- What is your current approach to language interpretation services? Do you have data to suggest your current approach is effective or sufficient?

- Do you have system-wide protocols in place for making certain all written materials produced are held to health literacy standards? Do you have uniform requirements for all written materials to be examined for cultural competence? Are all documents that are patient facing available in multiple languages? Is language interpretation available for written documents for patients whose preferred language is something other than those that are dominant in your service area?

- Have you developed a mechanism for making certain that patients who need interpretation services have those services provided throughout the continuum of their care?

CHAPTER EIGHT

COMMUNITY PARTNERSHIP

If you want to go quickly, go alone.
If you want to go far, go together.

—AFRICAN PROVERB

You cannot improve care for vulnerable communities unless you are an engaged, accepted participant in those communities. Yet the only sustainable way to improve health means helping patients become active partners in their care when they are *not* physically present in healthcare facilities. In order to address the social determinants of health, we must be actively involved in the places people live, work, and recreate. The best means to accomplish this end is to form partnerships with community institutions, groups, and individuals that emphasize outreach of health resources, promote health education, and provide prevention services. Partnering with places of worship, community service groups, schools, employers, and others creates bonds of trust between patients and health organizations.

One really useful model for how we at Northwell Health have attempted to maximize our engagement with community partners is a health worker training initiative we called "*From* the Community *for* the Community." The program was established to address an exploding need for middle-skill workers in the healthcare sector. Middle-skill occupations are jobs that do not require bachelor's degrees but require role-specific education and training beyond what is learned in high school, such as community health workers (CHWs), health coaches, and outreach associates. These positions pay a living wage, have opportunities for career advancement, and offer low-income families a pathway toward long-term economic dignity and security while providing their communities a tremendous resource.

One realization we've reached on our journey to improve diversity and inclusion is that patients and families are most effectively engaged and activated through meaningful relationships with healthcare workers from their own communities. Those employed in middle-skill healthcare occupations work alongside licensed providers as an integral part of the care team in order to help achieve outcomes that are meaningful to patients. As part of the public health workforce with ties to the local community, new legislation may permit many of these workers to be reimbursed by Medicaid for providing preventative services, if recommended by a licensed practitioner. This regulatory change creates a tremendous opportunity to integrate these positions into teams in order to improve care for underserved communities with complex medical needs.

Those who enrolled in our From the Community for the Community project completed an eight-week, skill-specific training curriculum and then entered into positions that largely focused on helping connect patients to community resources to continue their care after they had been discharged from our facilities. Previously, most of this work had been done by clinicians, so employees like our community health workers allowed us to free up clinical staff to concentrate on other duties while placing approachable faces in a community.

Several members of the Center for Equity of Care staff were devoted to the program, and when the first class graduated and had begun to settle into their new positions, one of our colleagues decided to bring participants together for lunch to check in with them and see how they were faring with their new responsibilities. At lunch, they talked about what they had encountered working in the community and discussed career path plans and opportunities. Nearly all the workers wished to continue their formal educations and advance in the health-care profession. At the conclusion of the lunch, our colleague offered one of the workers a ride back to the hospital in which she worked. This community health worker was someone he had conversed with several times before over the course of the program. Shortly after she got into his car, she started to cry. When our colleague inquired about what had upset her, she said she was embarrassed for him to see where she was living. She told him how incredibly grateful she was for the program and how fulfilling she found her work, but then she reluctantly revealed that she and her children were currently living in a homeless shelter. The shelter was a long way from the hospital, and she spent a lot of time on a bus getting to work, which only increased her worry about being able to get home at the end of the school day. She was under tremendous stress.

Our colleague saw a parent in distress, yet he recognized that she was not only intent on being the best possible parent she could be, but she also was deeply committed to her new role of helping the patients assigned to her. Her ability to support patients far exceeded the program's expectations, and she offered living evidence of how a community-focused program could be successful. Determined to find a way to change her family's circumstances, our colleague reached out to others at Northwell Health. We were able to get her family into an apartment owned by the health system and cover her rent for a period of time until she could get back on her feet. Northwell Health colleagues rallied around her family, donating items they needed for their apartment. With a hand up from people who cared for and respected her, our colleague was soon able to manage the apartment's rent. That success, in turn, gave her an even greater desire to continue her education and stay in the profession. This is a lived example of human connection and true community partnership.

REIGNITING HUMANISM THROUGH FORGING CONNECTIONS

When we introduced the community health worker program, we didn't fully recognize the magnitude or the complexity of the challenges faced by its participants and its patients. Our coworker's story is illustrative in many ways, for not only is her story one of tremendous success in how effective it is for such employees to serve their community as agents of healthcare continuity—directly targeting that eighty-twenty split between the social determinants of health and

The simple reality is that patients don't always tell clinicians the true story when it comes to their health.

clinical care—but it also reveals the vulnerability experienced by the members of the community the program was meant to serve. Simultaneously, she illustrates why community-based programs like this one work so well. The simple reality is that patients don't always tell clinicians the true story when it comes to their health. When patients meet with members of their community who look like them or live around the corner from them, they are willing to be more vulnerable and more revealing because they are less likely to feel judged. Because healthcare has historically been viewed as paternalistic, it's not unusual for patients to be suspicious of doctors or feel that they are misunderstood or judged. Community health workers meet with patients in their own homes or in community clinics, nonprofit facilities, or faith-based locations, and because community health workers are often familiar, patients are quicker to see them as partners in their care and are therefore more willing to pursue the health resources to which they are directed.

Consider the kinds of circumstances that community health workers commonly encounter, and you get a clearer picture of the dynamics between patients and their providers. Will the diabetes patient who is asked by their doctor to monitor their weight and glucose levels be willing to admit that they don't own a bathroom scale or cannot afford glucose test strips? Will the patient with high blood pressure be likely to receive a house call from their physician, let alone one that includes showing them the contents of their pantry?

Remember JR from the last chapter? Is he more likely to share his concerns over maintaining sexual intimacy in his relationship with his physician or with someone he sees as a peer?

It is difficult to fully understand either the assets or the disadvantages of the communities you serve unless you spend time in them. It is challenging to understand an individual's social determinants of health unless you are exposed to their daily lives. The time has come to refocus on partnerships with our communities.

This recognition is something that former US surgeon general Richard Carmona emphasized when he was the guest speaker at the tenth annual Northwell Health Summit on Diversity and Health Equity. Drawing on memories dating back to when Dr. Carmona was an army medic serving in Vietnam, he recalls learning how to earn the trust of Montagnard villagers by spending time in their villages and listening to the village leaders while sharing meals and swapping stories. Once trust was established by taking the time to learn their culture and lifestyle, Carmona received numerous lessons in developing cultural competency and health literacy, something he simply could not learn unless present.

Carmona tells the story of how, after being slowly vetted by the village chief to evaluate whether he could tend to the medical needs of the village, his first patient awaiting treatment was a little girl suffering from impetigo. He thought, "Well, this one will be easy and earn me some respect because all I need is to clean her up a bit and give her some penicillin." He gave the chief some soap, told him to have the girl wash with it several times a day, and then provided him with several dozen penicillin tablets and told him to give the girl one tablet four times a day. Dr. Carmona returned to the village two weeks later. Again, the first patient he saw was the little girl, and he was pleased to see the scabs had all fallen off and her skin was looking healthy.

To demonstrate their gratitude for his treating her and her fellow villagers, Carmona was presented with a Montagnard ring, a bracelet, and a ceremonial crossbow, items he has cherished all his life since that day, talismans of the lessons he learned there that he has carried forward into his career in public health. Then the villagers brought out a mahogany box, and upon opening it, he discovered a vine fashioned into a necklace. On the vine were forty penicillin pills. They thanked him for giving them the "beads" and explained how they had faithfully put one pill on the necklace four times a day for ten consecutive days. Proudly, they told him how they placed the necklace on any villager who was sick, believing in its power to make them better. Dr. Carmona, then a young medic, had thought he had accomplished so much good in the village, not just introducing medical solutions but communicating in a manner that they understood how the medical advancements of the West could bring them better health. He thought he had helped these remote people when he'd only reaped the benefit of serendipity. He had failed to accomplish health literacy. But he did depart with a lesson that would never leave him.

He had learned this lesson in an indelible way. And he'd learned more, for he realized that he had been a made an honored member of the village not because of his healing prowess but because he had taken the time and shown the respect to earn their trust. The lessons stayed with him. He applied them again and again as he approached healthcare disparities on Native American reservations, in poor urban communities like the one where he had grown up, and with the citizens of the New Orleans Ninth Ward in the aftermath of Hurricane Katrina. As he shared his story at a Northwell Health symposium, he emphasized lessons that we must learn: we must reach out through community institutions, those like faith communities and neighborhood organizations, connect to their leaders, and take the time

We have to meet community members where they live their lives, listen to them, share our mutual stories of love and hardship and pain and joy, mistakes and success.

necessary to gain people's trust. He reminds us to subordinate ourselves to the "village leaders"; in the eyes of the people, that leader is the person in charge, and they will follow the counsel the leader offers. Such simple wisdom can be guiding advice for how we begin to build partnerships with community organizations.

We cannot afford to be the professionals who arrive once a year for a health fair and depart. We have to meet community members where they live their lives, listen to them, share our mutual stories of love and hardship and pain and joy, mistakes and success. We have to break bread together. We must demonstrate to them that we are human and make certain that they see us not as a doctor or a social worker or community health worker but as another human being. Dr. Carmona counsels us to learn the cultures of those to whom we tend and embrace those cultures even if we disagree with their beliefs. Once we get inside and form bonds, only then can we have discussions. If we don't first acknowledge their beliefs, they will never trust us.[48]

Dr. Carmona's takeaways from his experiences echo ideas we have emphasized, that language access and education on health literacy are nested in a forming larger cultural competency. Cultural competency is best viewed as an ability to understand, communicate, and connect with the people you are serving. You can't attain cultural competency if you don't understand the community in which people live. Or, more accurately, the communities in which they live, for community is partly a physical location like our neighborhood and city, but more importantly and more personally, community is found in the people we spend our time with through our places of worship, schools, volunteer organizations, recreational teams, and the like. When health organizations partner with these kinds of community entities, we not only reach their participants, but we also have a better opportunity to increase our cultural competency. As Ram Raju, MD, a former senior vice president and community health investment officer of Northwell Health, said when researching lessons learned on how to best address issues of health disparities: "We had been looking at the seed—the person or patient. Now we started looking at the soil—where they live."[49] The story we shared about our community health worker embodies this approach.

We had been looking at the seed—the person or patient. Now we started looking at the soil—where they live.

—DR. RAM RAJU
Former Senior Vice President and Community Health
Investment Officer

Our investment in the From the Community for the Community program reveals many larger patterns for why community partnership by healthcare organizations can be such a powerful tool for eradicating health disparities that occur across racial, ethnic, socioeconomic, and cultural groups and for empowering people with tools and information to support healthy decision making. It's one of many such partnerships we have formed.

LEARNING TO REACH FOR HELP

In order to harness the power of community partnership, similar to what we did to determine our institutional readiness to best serve the needs of our diverse communities, Northwell Health first completed a comprehensive Community Health Needs Assessment (CHNA) from 2016 to 2019. This allowed us to identify and engage potential collaborative partners and seize on opportunities to develop sustainable and inclusive interventions to build a culture and community of health.

Our initiatives have targeted numerous specific segments of the communities we serve, often in innovative ways. Spinney Hill, less than half a mile from our flagship North Shore University Hospital, remains a community facing economic hardship. It is populated primarily by Black working-class residents who often felt neglected by its sprawling healthcare neighbor. Despite its proximity to the hospital, or more accurately, partly because of the largescale development of a huge academic hospital and all of the infrastructure that helps service it, Spinney Hill is an isolated residential neighborhood in a sea of development, one that is further isolated because it is bisected by Northern Boulevard, a major highway that is extremely dangerous for pedestrians to cross. While a vibrant community in many ways, in others, Spinney Hill is representative of communities that suffer economic and racial disparities that are surrounded by a culture of wealth. It is a neighborhood that cannot meet basic community needs because of an absence of a grocery store within a safe, walkable distance.

A pivotal moment in Northwell Health's relationship with the Spinney Hill neighborhood arrived when we sought yet another zoning approval for expansion. The community and the health system had reached a kind of standoff. Our Center for Equity of Care saw this as an opportunity and suggested to our leadership team that we would like to try and form a community coalition. We were able to take advantage of the fact that one of our team members was well-respected in Spinney Hill, and still, it took five meetings to get community members to realize that our interests in forming a partnership were genuine. Once we began working together, we identified three primary focus points: improving food security and nutrition education, educating on heart disease and stroke, and education on kidney disease. While data might have corroborated these community health emphasis points, we arrived at identifying them simply because we talked less and listened more, dropped assumptions and started learning. With a tenuous rapport established, we began to develop programs that addressed these concerns, including some food access programs that were aided by a grant provided by one of our trustees.

Sometimes small ventures in community engagement end up having an outsized impact. For example, we started a summer program working with local vendors from the North Island region at a farmer's market in the neighborhood. One of our teammates was a nutritionist. She worked with the nutrition team on recipes specifically aimed at the neighborhood and at the health concerns its members had expressed. Her team provided samples at the market and shared the recipes, building entire hot, healthy menus for people to enjoy. Eventually, the excitement over the food they presented got community members talking and sharing their own recipes and discussing their eating habits. Over time, one person would talk about losing weight, another would tell how they were able to get their diabetes under control through proper nutrition. From such inspiring stories and conversations, we were able to develop targeted educational programs and advertise them through the market. Those programs allowed us to come back and back again; they built friendships and relationships; they established trust. We began to be seen in the community as a collection of people who worked to better health rather than "those people from the hospital."

This approach is common to how we try to educate through meaningful community interaction and immersion. Northwell Health now runs teaching kitchens for the community at multiple locations. We also partner with Harlem Grown, a nonprofit which teaches healthy lifestyles through farm tending and a teaching kitchen. New York City's only hospital-based rooftop garden, offering nearly a hundred varieties of fruits, vegetables, and herbs from across the globe, can be found atop Lenox Hill Hospital in Greenwich Village.

A principle for what guides us in any community partnership is a commitment to meet people where they are, which includes trying to understand their living environments and their needs. We pay attention to what community members view as the factors that contribute to care disparity or that limit access. This approach is embodied in all the partnerships we form and includes our ability to create designated facilities that can offer focused expertise. This is the case with the Gerald J. Friedman Transgender Health & Wellness Program of Lenox Hill Hospital, which provides comprehensive medical services for the specialized needs of the transgender and nonbinary gender community. Lenox Hill Hospital works closely with the nearby LGBT Community Center in order to meet our patients' specific needs, just as Northwell Health partners with LGBTIA+ organizations near each of our hospitals. It is also the case with the Katz Institute for Women's Health (KIWH), which offers clinical services, education, and community programs, as well as women's health-focused research. Additionally, Northwell partners with the New York State Cancer Services Program to provide breast, cervical, and colorectal cancer screenings and diagnostic services at no cost to uninsured or underinsured community members. LIJ's Cancer Community Connection Program works to remove barriers to screening and treatment in Black and Latina women in Queens. The Rosen Family Wellness Center and the Mildred and Frank Feinberg

Division of the Unified Behavioral Health Center for Military Veterans and Their Families are dedicated to enhancing the well-being of military service members, 9/11 first responders, law enforcement personnel and their families. Among the programs developed through the center are Barracks to Business workshops, webinars, and job fairs to help translate military skills into career success. Health NYServes connects veterans to more than sixty service providers.

We could fill a substantial portion of this book simply chronicling the community outreach and partnership programs Northwell has developed. Despite that fact, we regard community partnerships as the pillar that still requires the most growth. We've shared these glimpses at just a few of our efforts to suggest some of the ways that we reach purposefully into meeting the needs of diverse populations. But what should you take away from these short introductions? For starters, let's return to that idea of meeting people where they are at. Not only do we differentiate the needs of distinct community members, but our default position also is always to think in terms of a global approach that empowers people, educates them, and maximizes the potential impact on their long-term health.

With community partnerships, we also default toward prevention and wellness over acute care in recognition that an ability to alter social determinants of health favorably has amplified results that tend to create ever-growing impacts on other segments of the community and that promote change for future generations. While, for example, sometimes it is appropriate simply to solve the immediate short-term food needs of a population, lasting impact comes when you partner with a food pantry that, in addition to providing nutritious food, also runs programs that educate people about how to grow and cook food and how to plan nutritious meals. A teaching kitchen does far more than fill a hungry belly; it also provides people tools and spawns fledgling entrepreneurs who then start food trucks and farm-to-table-themed eateries. Helping a disabled veteran find gainful employment in the healthcare sector can have as many positive health effects as can treating their chronic condition. We've seen how helping a valuable colleague find a secure living environment not only allows her to continue the education that will grow her career, but it also may provide a vital step toward a better future for her children.

MEET PEOPLE WHERE THEY ARE

Being present in our communities via partnerships with organizations that are familiar to people helps us build trust in those communities. Frequently, we administer community health screenings, host patient support groups, and provide health education classes within faith-based organizations. Our BERGs often play a significant role in engaging trusted partnerships with our communities. When we gain the support of pastors, rabbis, priests, and imams, the outreach programs we administer give a community megaphone to which people listen, just as Dr. Carmona had instructed. When such programs are held in a physical space that is familiar and holds personal meaning to the participants, they regard such resources as accessible and comfortable. It's human nature, after all, to seek comfort in the familiar among others we know and who share a lot in common with us.

Meeting people where they are also means listening to their needs rather than dictating what you preconceive to be their priorities. Partnerships and trust develop when our patients share in the decision in the comfort of their own homes. As evidenced by our successful Health House Calls Program, which provides home-based advanced illness management for homebound patients, through which 78 percent of patients were treated successfully at home with no need for hospitalization. This kind of approach promotes self-efficacy. Helping community programs that assist their neighbors in transforming their businesses and homes to be ADA compliant changes people's lives in ways that allow them to be more mobile, more engaged with others, and better able to access the services that can improve their daily lives. When we participate in education and access programs, we not only help people become more self-reliant, but they also begin to take greater responsibility for their health.

Like with all the work we do, the pillars of how we address disparity in healthcare are reciprocal. For example, it's largely through our partnerships with faith-based community organizations that we were able to educate community members on our "We Ask Because We Care" initiative. This campaign aims to educate both our team members and community members about the importance of collecting and using accurate race, ethnicity and preferred language data. Without community understanding of the importance of such data, people can misunderstand our use of it and not understand why accurate patient information helps make exceptional care possible.

If we go back to our colleague's story that opened this chapter, its message, both in the motivation she felt to provide care to her community and in the heartache we felt at learning a colleague faced such hardship, is about an essential human desire to ease another's burden. This community health worker found her calling in healthcare in a way not that different from how Dr. Richard Carmona found his—by sitting face to face with another person, by sharing a meal, by swapping stories. The instincts they acted upon are as old as humanity itself. When we learn to take the spirit of such encounters and develop systematic outreach into the communities where people live their lives, we can form powerful partnerships that can transform people's social determinants of health.

WHAT ARE THE NEXT STEPS ON YOUR JOURNEY TOWARD HEALTH EQUITY?

- Share a story from within your organization for when a spontaneous or happenchance community encounter led to the creation of a formal partnership.

- Share a story from your organization where an essential truth about the relationship between place, community, and health was revealed to you.

- Can you identify communities in your area that are severely underserved or that have poor healthcare access? What leaders and what organizations do you have connections with whom you might partner?

- Do you have specific partnerships formed with organizations that represent niche and minority community members in the area you serve?

- Do your service area demographics support particular faith-based communities that have leverage in their followers' lives?

CHAPTER NINE

SUPPLIER DIVERSITY

The test of our progress is not whether we add more to the abundance of those who have much; it is whether we provide enough for those who have too little.

—FRANKLIN D. ROOSEVELT

To truly transform healthcare access for those from historically underrepresented populations, community outreach and education programs have to be coupled with the creation of economic opportunities aimed at leveling the playing field. Supporting local minority, women, and LGBTQIA+ owned businesses with coordinated direct financial support, education, and

---

assistance in networking can have an expansive, even and exponential, impact on numerous people's lives. The more business a healthcare system can conduct with local entities, the greater its impact on the total health of its communities and the more lasting effect it can have on improving the social determinants of health. Twenty-first-century medicine means also paying attention to where and how we source supplies.

Andy Posner, founder and CEO of Capital Good Fund, suggests that we should amend the old proverb about "teach a man to fish" to instead read: "Give a woman a fish, and she'll have the energy to take care of her children, do well at work, and pursue her goals. Teach her to fish and give her access to a pond full of fish, and she'll be able to feed herself and her family for life."[50] His modification of the adage recognizes that while education is immensely important to changing economic capacity, education alone is insufficient to create lasting change. It has to be coupled with opportunity, access, and a level playing field. That recognition is applicable to the way in which supporting local businesses with coordinated direct financial support, education, and assistance in networking can have an expansive impact on numerous people's lives. Such recognition is at the heart of why we believe that increasing supplier diversity must be a central pillar to helping lift our communities and improve the health of the people who live in them.

The same Communication Climate Assessment Tool (CCAT) survey that revealed how poor of a job we were doing to provide language access to our patients also demonstrated the stark reality that people in our surrounding communities often felt disconnected from our health system. Among them were many business owners. Some lamented that as Northwell Health grew, its size meant that it looked outside the region and often outside the United States as it secured supply procurements and courted vendors. Too often, we were trading with giant corporations rather than nearby mom-and-pop shops. Northwell Health was serious about its commitment to form partnerships in the communities it served. But as we took a closer look, we were embarrassed how few of our suppliers were businesses owned by women, people of color, LGBTQIA+, veterans, people with disabilities, and others who make up our expansive view of diversity. We didn't reflect the faces of the communities we served among those with whom we did business for goods and services.

While developing what would become the American Hospital Association's (AHA's) Equity of Care Pledge, committee members discussed the importance of developing layered, sustainable community partnerships and saw supplier diversity as a key means to demonstrate commitment to such partnerships by investing in the community. Recognizing the AHA's vision and seeing the results of the CCAT survey, we set about developing a strategic plan for trying to build diverse supplier relationships. All of our experiences told us that to accomplish such goals, we would have to go beyond forming the kinds of community partnerships we discussed in the previous chapter and make it clear that we wished to invest in the long-term economic health of our communities. Our realization that trust-based, lasting partnerships with community members required economic investment is a direct extension of the holistic view we hold for what it takes for more people to achieve their health goals.

As we began to develop a strategic plan for expanding supplier diversity, we reached out to peer healthcare systems to learn more about their best practices. There weren't many others in the sector that were active in such partnership, though we took guidance where we found it, particularly from Kaiser Permanente and from the Henry Ford Health System. Largely, the supplier diversity element of inclusion and equity programs was in its fledgling stages. As a result, we have broken a lot of new ground in this space. To help find our bearings as we trail blazed, we also sought out advice beyond the health sector, including asking Rohini Anand, the former senior vice president and global chief diversity officer of Sodexo, to vet our plan. Among other suggestions, Anand reinforced the need to take a multipronged approach to achieve health equity, including an emphasis on the role of community investment.

RIPPLES IN THE WATER

Our institutional size—in workforce, in physical facilities, and in individuals served—provides Northwell Health a unique opportunity to leverage the power of economic investment. Of course, our supply needs are vast, so the scale we needed meant utilizing corporations big enough to meet demands at effective price points. The pressure to work with corporations sizable enough to promote savings becomes even greater when you operate, as we do, on 1 or 2 percent margins. But along the way, we had lost sight of the interwoven economic impacts that can change an entire community when we keep a portion of supply needs more local.

When we invest in businesses within the communities we serve, that investment flows through those businesses into the wallets of their employees and their families. Smart community investment has a multiplier effect, like the ripples broadcast outward from an object dropped into water. Growth in one business can generate secondary investment with subcontractors, parts suppliers, and business partners.

When we invest in businesses within the communities we serve, that investment flows through those businesses into the wallets of their employees and their families.

More money in the hands of those in the community can create more opportunities for small service-oriented businesses to rise up and for more reinvestment in things like housing improvement. Greater spending increases tax revenue in the municipalities where those businesses and their employees are located, which in turn can spark infrastructure improvements that better public spaces and public institutions. Such an approach is similar to that taken by Andy Posner and Capital Good Fund, which has used microloans and other investments in poor farming communities around the globe to spark economic growth.

Community economic investment can have a sweeping and sustainable impact. By studying supplier diversity initiatives in our peer institutions and among other industries, we've witnessed such economic principles in action through our own initiatives and pilot projects. Just as too many people have long been underrepresented within the institutions that determine how their health needs are met, too many minority business owners have faced an inequitable disadvantage in establishing and scaling businesses. Health organizations gain value by creating opportunities as well. The suppliers who do business in our communities are also our patients. Doing business with them shifts how we are perceived by those patients and creates an advantage over our competitors.

GROWING SUPPLIER DIVERSITY

In an attempt to bring balanced access to opportunity, the Center for Equity of Care, in partnership with the Northwell Health Office of Procurement, has redefined and enhanced Northwell's supplier diversity program. Northwell is a member of the Minority Supplier Development Council (NY/NJ), a global leader in advancing business opportunities for its certified Asian, Black, Hispanic, and Native American business enterprises and connecting them to member corporations. Northwell Health evaluates potential vendors within categories and product-specific needs defining three schemata—quality of product/service and fulfillment of patient and Northwell's needs; cost mitigation; and alignment with the strategic vision, including the promotion of diversity and inclusion.

What we have discovered is a wealth of untapped potential. This phenomenon is not specific to our service area. The *Harvard Business Review* recently noted that:

> *The U.S. Small Business Administration estimates there were eight million minority-owned companies in the United States as of 2018. The National Minority Supplier Diversity Council reports that certified minority business enterprises generate $400 billion in economic output that led to the creation or preservation of 2.2 million jobs and $49 billion in annual revenue for local, state, and federal tax authorities. And those numbers are steadily increasing.*[51]

That such impact is growing is certainly good news. But how many minority entrepreneurs have not had the opportunity to start a business? How many have failed because they could not secure contracts with sizable clients? How many face limited profits and limited hiring because their corporate neighbors overlook them?

One of the first steps we took to fulfill this need was to work with our procurement office. With their help, we formed a council, which immediately set about developing the guidelines and the processes for local and regional businesses to be able to work with us. We joined the Healthcare Supplier Diversity Alliance, which continues to provide us a rich resource for studying best practices in this space and to meet key stakeholders across the healthcare supply chain. At Northwell Health, we are explicit and intentional in reaching out to diverse suppliers, and we have solidified our commitment to supplier diversity by mandating that 30 percent of our contracts have to be with minority-, women-, veteran-, LGBTQIA+, and disability-owned businesses. By developing detailed requirements for bid processes across all types of vendors, whether they are a medical equipment supplier or an executive coaching vendor and everything in between, we have made certain that all those we look to do business with are held to the same standards.

From there, we developed a number of related programs operating on the same principles, including establishing a Global Health Initiatives Advisory Board that works to maximize positive impact on reducing disparities in healthcare within the organization's national and international communities. We also partnered with MedShare, an organization that recovers valuable, unused surplus medical supplies and equipment that would be otherwise discarded. By giving new life to medical supplies, we can help link sustainability initiatives to supply chain solutions, which reflects the kinds of innovations we often find among our diverse suppliers. They tend to be a resilient and creative segment of businesses because the simple truth is that they are accustomed to working harder to achieve success in environments that have often erected far too many hurdles. These qualities make for great partners that tend to bring a great deal more value than the goods and services they provide to Northwell Health.

I believe there is strength through diversity. Northwell Health's commitment to doing business with diverse suppliers strengthens our supply chain, promotes innovation, and reinforces our dedication to the economic growth of the communities we serve.

—PHYLLIS MCCREADY
Senior Vice President and Chief Procurement Officer

MEASURING RESULTS

We collect data on supplier diversity for all our contracts, including those from Tier 1 suppliers (those we contract with directly for supplies or services) and from Tier 2 suppliers (those Tier 1 suppliers work with to fulfill their contracts). As has been our approach throughout, we recognize that without data, we cannot measure results. Having evidence of success is critical for getting leadership buy-in. When we can demonstrate hard data that illustrates how successful such relationships can prove, it helps us recruit new suppliers as well. In our case, in 2020, we increased minority spend by 18.6 percent and women-owned spend by 5.31 percent; combined, in that year, our diverse spending totaled $92,012,156.

Of course, the data focused on spending is limited in what it can reveal. Spend data can't tell you if your suppliers are also encouraging inclusion in their workforce and sub-suppliers. In that instance, analyzing a supplier's workforce makeup is also part of what Northwell Health studies before investing. Additionally, we wish to measure the impacts of a supplier relationship to other parts of the community, so we gather a great deal of Tier 2 data, learning more about those suppliers and their presence as employers in our communities through quarterly reporting.

When we link data to anecdotal success stories that we present at symposiums and workshops, people pay attention and take pride in seeing businesses in their community thrive. As always, we work to link narrative—the stories of lives changed because of policy initiatives—to data. Once we get vendors talking to other vendors, then that community investment can really begin to pay dividends.

A FOCUS ON PEERS AND MENTORS

Sharing the experiences suppliers have when working with Northwell Health is something that we have been proactive about developing. We are intentional in educating our suppliers and partners: bringing them in for meetings, spending time with them, fostering relationships, getting them to know Northwell Health's values and processes. We also capitalize on our strengths as educators. By encouraging relationships among suppliers, we are able to help expand their skills and knowledge so that they can better meet Northwell Health's needs while also developing their ability to innovate, forge other business relationships, and generally do what they already do well even better. Sometimes that is accomplished through certifications or through formal education programs and workshops, and other times it's done simply by bringing different suppliers together and creating an atmosphere where they can learn from one another. For example, every year, we host a healthcare symposium with the New York/New Jersey Minority Supplier Development Council that brings in hundreds of Northwell Health partners and use a kind of speed dating format where they get a chance to practice elevator pitches. We then try to match our needs with what the businesses that attend can offer. They gain insights into our procurement processes and get to know some of our leadership.

Simultaneously, we foster opportunities for existing suppliers to talk with prospective ones. This allows suppliers to develop informal mentorship programs, passing along their experiences and expertise.

Perhaps the most important thing we have learned in developing supplier diversity at Northwell Health is to remember that the businesses with which we work are owned and operated by people who have lived lives full of diverse experiences.

This also applies to Tier 1 suppliers interacting with Tier 2 suppliers in settings where Northwell Health is their host, which allows smaller, often younger companies to learn mechanisms for growing their businesses.

At the core of all these mentorships, partnerships, and collegial friendships are human faces. Every business, large and small, is successful because it has been founded, led, and built by unique, vibrant people. Perhaps the most important thing we have learned in developing supplier diversity at Northwell Health is to remember that the businesses with which we work are owned and operated by people who have lived lives full of diverse experiences. Their experiences have helped them develop individualized perspectives—on business and on health. Each of them has, in turn, developed vital relationships with their employees and fellow community members. Whether it is creating an alliance with a religious leader, a community activist, a government figure, or a local businessperson, success in those relationships has an exponential impact on the community because they touch so many lives. In the case of partnering with local business leaders, their impact can be more exponential still because they can have such an influence on how financial resources can flow through a community and therefore can create a disproportionate contribution to the total health of those communities.

WHAT ARE THE NEXT STEPS ON YOUR JOURNEY TOWARD HEALTH EQUITY?

- Share a story from within your organization in which one of your diverse suppliers has had a ripple effect for improving community economic development.

- What percentage of your total supplier spend comes from minority business enterprises, women-, veteran-, disabled-, or LGTBQIA+ owned businesses?

- What peer-to-peer mechanisms do you have in place for informal mentoring, discussion, and coordination specific to your suppliers?

- Do you have councils, committees, or BERGs that work directly with suppliers to familiarize them on opportunities to work with your organization or to share processes and procedures used by your organization?

- Does your organization have a structured mechanism for encouraging and/or financing innovative development of products and services by suppliers and/or employees?

CHAPTER TEN

WORKFORCE

Human communities depend upon a diversity of talent, not a singular conception of ability. And at the heart of the challenge is to reconstitute our sense of ability and intelligence.

—KEN ROBINSON

Large organizations are complex ecosystems. In order to maintain the healthiest, most verdant, most sustainable healthcare ecosystem, you need a workforce loaded with diverse ideas and fresh perspectives, one that reflects and understands the community it serves. You also need institutional infrastructure in place to make those diverse ideas, and fresh perspectives are shared, discussed, and presented to your leadership team, a team that also needs to reflect the diversity of your community and your patient population. Neither of these two goals can be accomplished unless you create a workplace culture that allows team members to be their authentic selves.

There's a frequent plotline in movies where the protagonist arrives at a party, and he or she is the only one who is the only one wearing a costume. Maybe you've even experienced such a scenario. In the movies, the faux pas has usually happened because the protagonist is being bullied, and someone wants them to feel embarrassed. But what's it like to continuously be in business meetings or on rounds where you're made to feel out of place or uniquely visible? This is the daily experience for far too many women or people of color or disabled individuals. This is hardly a funny plot line or a bit of passing embarrassment. It's also not an experience reflective of the larger demographics of the US population. Women of color account for 38.3 percent of the female civilian labor force, yet only 4.7 percent of executive- or senior-level officials and managers in S&P 500 companies.[52] In 2021, *Fortune* published an article celebrating milestones for female CEOs in its Fortune 500 list; while the records they heralded were real, their fanfare was sparked by the appearance of *forty-one* women on its list of *five hundred* companies; that's just over 8 percent, by the way.[53] Healthcare leadership data hasn't shifted significantly since a 2015 benchmark study (the most recent year for which data has been published) where the AHA Institute for Diversity and Health Equity showed that while minorities made up 32 percent of patients, they held 11 percent of executive leadership positions at hospitals.[54]

Beyond the vacuum of missing diversity among healthcare leaders, far too often, those in marginalized groups disproportionately make up the healthcare occupations that offer the lowest pay. Racial and ethnic diversity in many healthcare professions has not kept pace with demographic changes in the general populations of the United States. Healthcare is still an industry where 56.2 percent of active physicians are White, while 5.8 percent are Hispanic, and 5 percent are Black.[55] Compare that with the numbers for personal care aides, where Hispanics account for 18.2 percent of the workforce and Blacks for 22.1 percent.[56] Chiropractors, speech-language pathologists, veterinarians, audiologists, and podiatrists have some of the lowest proportions of professionals of color. Here are some additional insights on the healthcare workforce:

- Hispanic populations are significantly underrepresented in all of the occupations affiliated with diagnosing medical conditions and among treating practitioners.

- Among non-Hispanics, Blacks are underrepresented in all occupations, except among dieticians and nutritionists (15.0 percent) and respiratory therapists (12.8 percent).

- Asians are underrepresented among speech-language pathologists (2.2 percent) and advanced practice registered nurses (4.1 percent).

- American Indians and Alaska Natives are underrepresented in all occupations except physician assistants and have the lowest representation among physicians and dentists (0.1 percent in each occupation).

These sizable gaps of diversity can translate into communication breakdowns, limited perspectives, lack of role models, lack of future diversity, and the festering presence of implicit bias.

*These sizable gaps of diversity can translate into
communication breakdowns, limited perspectives,
lack of role models, lack of future diversity,
and the festering presence of implicit bias.*

To help avoid such concerns, the goal is pretty simple to state: to have a workforce that reflects the community it serves. It's a lot harder to accomplish. As a leader in the healthcare industry serving multicultural communities, Northwell Health is committed to fostering equity, diversity, and inclusion within our health network so that we may better serve our patient population. Our goals of sustaining diverse and inclusive team member recruitment, development, and advancement help us ensure that our team members represent the communities we serve and also have opportunities to realize their full potential. An inclusive workforce allows us to deliver culturally appropriate patient care as evidenced through our team member engagement scores and patient satisfaction data.

MORE DIVERSITY = BETTER OUTCOMES

You may see having a diverse workforce as a noble goal, but it's far more than an area of emphasis that reflects our values; there are direct benefits we gain as a health system. The shortfalls we have detailed are embarrassing really, particularly when recognizing that the presence of a diverse healthcare workforce has quite direct repercussions for patients and the quality of patient care. Indeed, diversity in the workplace carries a host of benefits for healthcare employers, their staff, and their patients. Those benefits include:

- Having a healthcare staff as diverse as the patient base they are treating helps ensure that there is someone on staff who can identify with the patient, communicate with them, and better serve their individual needs.

- Diversity creates a stronger feeling of inclusion and community for healthcare workers, which makes the workplace feel safer and more enjoyable.

- Inclusion and community increase team member retention. This goes hand in hand with improved morale, a distinguishing trait in a work environment where people feel happy and safe.

- A commitment to diversity helps when recruiting new healthcare workers and administrative staff. This allows employers to cast a wider net to attract new talent, and it offers a stronger hiring proposition for strong candidates.

- The new ideas and varied perspectives that emerge from a diverse workforce can lead to greater innovation and operational excellence.

A diverse bouquet of voices inspires better discussions, better decisions, and better outcomes for everyone.

On the patient outcome front, not only are patient desires clear, but the results on patient outcomes can also be quite striking. "Racial and ethnic minority patients who have a choice are more likely to select health care professionals of their own racial or ethnic background."[57] Moreover, when treated by a health professional of their own race or ethnic background, patients are generally more satisfied with their care and are more likely to report receiving higher-quality care.[58] One study in 2019 that compared Black male patients treated by Black doctors or Black health professionals versus Black male patients treated by non-Black doctors or health professionals produced findings that suggest Black doctors could reduce the Black-White gap in cardiovascular mortality for males by 19 percent.[59] Black male patients showed increased comfort in fully discussing their healthcare problems with Black doctors, and Black doctors/HCPs wrote more additional notes about their patients' cases and spent more time with the Black male patients, largely because their Black patients agreed to more potentially life-saving screenings.[60]

Need more evidence? Wherever diversity is encouraged and cultivated, businesses (hospitals included) perform significantly better:

- A study by the firm McKinsey and Company found that gender-diverse companies are 15 percent more likely to outperform non-gender-diverse companies, and ethnically diverse companies are 35 percent more likely to outperform companies with minimal diversity.[61]

- Diversity even has an effect *before* a medical worker enters the field. Studies have shown that students who study within a diverse student body and faculty make better doctors. A 2008 study by the David Geffen School of Medicine at UCLA found that "student diversity in medical education is a key component in creating a physician workforce that can best meet the needs of an increasingly diverse population and could be a tool in helping to end disparities in health and healthcare."[62]

In short, the numbers tell us that diversity leads to happier patients, more content team members, and better medical results.

These studies and others lend support for a simple truth we have focused on throughout the book: when patients are in healthcare environments where they feel comfortable and understood, they become more active agents in their own care. Greater diversity in the healthcare workforce is seen as a promising strategy for addressing racial and ethnic healthcare disparities by improving access to healthcare for underserved patients, improving the patient experience, and increasing patient satisfaction.

FOSTERING AN INTERNAL CULTURE OF INCLUSION

Building an inclusive and diverse healthcare workforce takes work and commitment. One good starting point is to remember that your organization's employees are also patients of that system. As the list of attributes that accompany a diverse workforce make clear, the goals of making a health organization the trusted choice for your patients go hand in hand with making it one where people want to work. Northwell Health wants to be identified in the communities we serve as the best place in those communities to work. Northwell Health is a member of the national Democracy Collaborative, which leverages our substantial economic footprint by increasing our local hiring and encourages local businesses to invest in our institutions.

The goals of making a health organization the trusted choice for your patients go hand in hand with making it one where people want to work.

Inclusion in the workplace will continue to be a vital component in the future. In order for diversity programs and initiatives to be successful, organizations have to be inclusive. Diversity does not exist without inclusion. When employees feel included, they feel a sense of belonging that drives increased positive performance results and creates collaborative teams that are innovative. Employees who feel included are more likely to be positively engaged within the organization. Higher employee engagement drives higher levels of productivity, retention, and a company's overall success. Employees should feel a sense of belonging in the places they work. Engagement, diversity, inclusion, and belonging all coincide with one another.

Northwell Health's framework for upholding the organization's mission, values, and behavioral expectations is called the Culture of CARE. Our acronym CARE stands for Connectedness, Awareness, Respect, and Empathy. All four terms should sound familiar from our earlier discussion describing what inclusion in the workplace looks like. CARE is further reflected in our employee promise: "Made for this." Together, all of our employees own the culture of Northwell Health and believe the culture is theirs to shape. Our team members bring individuality to how they care for people—their patients, their community, and each other. The employee promise reflects that every member of our workforce is unique, yet all are part of a greater whole, both aspects of an inclusive vision that applies the allied spirit of working toward a common goal. The pursuit of diversity, inclusion, and equity is a philosophy that permeates all that we do.

Among our objectives for making Northwell Health the best and most welcoming workplace possible, we make certain that diversity and inclusion are considered essential to attracting the most talented employees from the widest talent pools. From there, we work to ensure that we utilize an unbiased lens in our workforce strategies, processes, and programs to help develop, advance, and retain our team members. To accomplish those objectives also means prioritizing inclusive leadership and increasing leadership diversity. We undertake approaches that work both top down (like increasing leadership diversity) and bottom up (like creating mechanisms for all employees to discuss their ideas and visions through mechanisms like our BERGS simultaneously). The result is the development of fair employment practices that have created a caring, inclusive culture that in turn generates a dynamic, innovative workforce. The intentional presence of diverse visions builds resiliency throughout the organization.

Central to our workforce infrastructure are our BERGs. The Northwell Health BERG program was established to enhance employee engagement, innovation, and talent development and promote an inclusive culture ensuring the delivery of culturally sensitive, quality patient care. Each of our BERGs targets different populations or employee interests—allies for our interests—and not only do they provide employees a sounding board for sharing ideas and team-oriented problem solving, but they also are active throughout the organization and within the community creating initiatives to further the interests they represent. For example, VALOR, our BERG for veterans, runs programs like "Barracks to Business," which conducts job fairs, workshops, hiring events, and mentorship programs aimed at helping veterans find meaningful careers at Northwell Health. Our N-Able BERG hosts an annual Disability Pride Conference that celebrates the contributions and unique talents of individuals with disabilities and provides education and resources to employees who are also care providers for people with disabilities. These are just two examples of literally hundreds of outreach programs and initiatives developed by our BERGs. What they illustrate is how meaningfully active and proactive our BERGS are. While they hold important connections to oversight and governance structures and have a voice in policy making at Northwell Health, they are equally focused on actively creating change and offering support to our employees.

Through purely voluntary employee participation, our BERGs are integral to fulfilling our mission. They serve an important role in building a diverse pipeline of talent at all levels and cultivate sustainable trusted partnerships with the communities we serve. A 2019 Employee Engagement survey we conducted revealed that 90 percent of our BERG members saw the value in diversity activities and believed Northwell Health values employees from different backgrounds.

BERG objectives include developing employee engagement and serving as ambassadors and allies to minorities, women, people with disabilities, veterans and individuals who identify as LGBTQIA+. BERG initiatives lead to high-quality patient care and overall community wellness. They are critical to enhancing talent recruitment and retention. As an integral component of our diversity and health equity strategy, our BERGs create a mentoring and sponsorship culture by recognizing, inspiring, and fostering high potential talent and cultivate education, allyship, respect, and inclusion within the workplace.

At Northwell Health, we have seven BERGs, which have more than five thousand members:

- **VALOR: Veterans and Allies Liaisons of Reintegration.** Members are dedicated to serving our military personnel, veterans, and their family members. Teams work with service members to connect them with resources that support their physical and psychological well-being and our talent development and recruitment programs.

- **Expressions.** Members consist of individuals who identify as LGBTQIA+, are allies of the LGBTQIA+ community, and are passionate about promoting unity and health equity. They promote awareness and inclusion in the workplace and connect the community with services based on their unique healthcare needs.

- **Bridges.** Members are passionate about cultural diversity and embrace relationship building through understanding and supporting the cultural, spiritual, and ethical values of the communities we serve. Market segments include Asian, African American / Caribbean, Jewish, and Latinx communities.

- **N-able.** Members are committed to connecting individuals with disabilities to the right healthcare resources and services. Members also serve as educators for employees, hiring leaders, healthcare professionals, and the community at large around issues of acceptance and inclusion.

- **GreenBERG.** Members are focused on the environmental impact of Northwell Health's operations. They leverage sustainable and socially responsive initiatives in the workplace and in our communities, with a focus on recycling, transportation, and energy efficiency.

- **Women in Healthcare.** Members connect and inspire women by providing opportunities for advocacy, community service, and development. All team members who are committed to advancing diversity, inclusion, and health equity are encouraged to join this BERG.

- **DLEN: Donate Life Employee Network.** Members help inspire others to give the gift of life through organ, tissue, and eye donation. They raise awareness among colleagues and community members to ultimately increase organ donor registrations in New York.

These seven BERGs, individually and collectively, do indispensable work. They are our eyes and our ears, not only within the workforce but within the larger community. Because they are so deeply connected to those for whom they advocate, you can't always predict the intervention mechanisms for how their work has an impact. Some come from intentional outreach, others from simply being present in the community with open ears. For example, consider the anecdote we shared illustrating the importance of cultural sensitivity about how Korean women were not selecting the Katz Institute for Women's Health as their childbirth destination despite it having opened a multimillion-dollar state-of-the-art birthing center. It was through the trust established by our Bridges BERG members that the Katz Institute learned women stayed away in large part because they did not serve *miyeok guk* (seaweed soup), which is a postpartum staple in Korean childbirth. Without BERG members, it is entirely likely that the Katz Institute would never have solved this little mystery and known that some simple changes could help change the perception of a sizable patient population.

Sometimes the benefits of having team members focused on improving care for patients can be small in scale and remedied with simple solutions, and sometimes they can be grand, but they always begin with human-to-human interaction. The above anecdote is a vital reminder of what "meeting the patient where they are at" can look like. No doubt your community and your workforce have different faces than ours, but if you align community and workforce interests and you create a specific mechanism for communication and the exchange of ideas, you can create the means to transform patient care while also making your organization be the workplace people *want* to work. The essential laws of supply and demand demonstrate that the more attractive your health organization becomes for potential employees, the more you can attract those who will excel. Our BERGs often provide a direct pipeline for identifying and retaining extraordinary talent.

Similar to the role played by our BERGs, we have established numerous leadership councils to provide oversight and guidance on diversity and health equity initiatives and to promote organizational change. Such councils provide a mechanism for our leaders to make good on their stated obligation to make diversity and inclusion an organizational priority and listen to team members, promote education, embrace transparency, and lead by example. Seven different councils with a combined leader membership of more than three hundred from all segments of the health system focus on health equity objectives from differing perspectives. Whether focused on effective education, supplier diversity, physician perspectives, or other vital needs, each council shares best practices and fosters collaboration. Their existence ensures that our organizational mission statement and values aren't just words on a page but action items for creating and sustaining change.

We invest in these forms of organizational structure and in the advancement of health equity because we are cognizant that the presence of diverse perspectives makes the organization stronger and more competitive. Diversity and inclusion foster innovation, which is the lifeblood of any enterprise. Extending opportunities to those who might be otherwise overlooked can result in fresh perspectives and real solutions. Northwell Health has long placed a premium on innovation, which gave rise to Northwell Ventures, an investment arm of the health system, and to the Innovation Challenge. The Innovation Challenge provides any Northwell Health employee who has an idea that can generate additional revenue through new or existing channels with the opportunity to receive up to $500,000 in funding and to partner in a new business venture. Such initiatives reflect a culture where people from throughout the system are encouraged to apply creative problem solving.

One person who embodies this entrepreneurial spirit is Lorenz "Buddy" Mayer, a sanitation administrator at North Shore University Hospital, who, over a thirty-year career, worked his way up from his first job as a hospital custodian. After receiving calls from clinicians concerned about the potential spread of infection to patients from privacy curtains—those cloth cubicle dividers that are ubiquitous in hospitals—Mayer began observing how employees handled the curtains and started reading literature that was emerging about how rapidly they became contaminated with potentially pathogenic bacteria. Cubicle dividers cannot be washed in place, and the process of removing and replacing curtains and sending them off-site for washing takes about an hour. Through his observations, Buddy saw that staff nearly always handled the curtains in the same place, which left him wondering if a solution might be as simple as it seemed. He developed a prototype by working with the curtain supplier, creating a vinyl attachment that could be rapidly cleaned on the spot with solutions already being used in those facilities. The Hand Shield was born. Northwell Ventures, working through the Feinstein Institute's Office of Technology Transfer, applied for a patent and then oversaw the development of the product. In a five-year period, sales of the Hand Shield are expected to generate $1.3 million. Not bad for a poor farm kid who, growing up, hired himself out to kill rats for his neighbors to earn money for his family. Under the Northwell Ventures agreement, Buddy is entitled to 40 percent of the profits for the Hand Shield. Buddy didn't set out to make money on his innovation; his real interest was in helping stop the spread of infections. Because of the open-minded, supportive spirit of employment at Northwell Health, his good idea has become a tremendous tool that enhances patient safety.

WORKFORCE STRATEGIES TO FOSTER AND SUSTAIN A CULTURE OF INCLUSION

What are some concrete strategies that can help you develop an engaged, empowered workforce who might take the kinds of initiative embodied by Buddy's story? Here are some you must put in place in order to be successful:

Hire diverse talent. Source and hire culturally competent, diverse talent, so team members are representative of our communities and patients. Northwell Health's focus includes sourcing, diverse slate, and diverse interview panels.

Unbiased career experience. Ensure unbiased development, advancement programs and processes that provide all team members the opportunity to achieve their career aspirations, including advancement, succession, and mentorship/development opportunities.

Fair total rewards practices. Ensure fair and inclusive total rewards practices to support all team members. Initiatives include leave, pay equity, flexible work opportunities, and caregiver support.

Develop culturally competent and inclusive leaders. Educate leaders on diversity, inclusion, and equity competencies to incorporate into their decisions, processes, and team culture.

Foster an inclusive culture. Foster a culture where all team members are heard, feel valued, and belong. Develop or expand structural governance and employee participation groups like BERGs to utilize their diverse perspective on workforce diversity, inclusion, and equity initiatives and business decisions. At Northwell Health, we have launched an Inclusion Academy to focus on education for all team members that includes unconscious bias, sexual harassment prevention, respectful work environment and inclusion/civility/allyship training.

Create a sustainable diversity and inclusion structure. Align strategies and structures, and develop resources and communications necessary for success. Initiatives include utilizing demographic and qualitative metrics to help inform decision making for increased and accelerated diverse and inclusive hiring, development and advancement.

All these sorts of strategies are rooted in a human desire to connect with people as present in our vision of an engaged workforce. This spirit of belief and investment in people is at the heart of Northwell Health's approach. It is built on a simple realization: people want to work where they and their ideas are respected and they feel heard. It just so happens that an environment that supports diversity

*People want to work where they and their ideas
are respected and they feel heard.*

also makes innovation more likely to flourish. Every workplace is full of people like Buddy, who, provided opportunity, seize it. Creating opportunities, including the opportunity for people to feel respected and included, is the essential mindset of those fighting for diversity and inclusion. Buddy offers one individual example of how an employee with a good idea can act on making the daily experience of patients safer and employee's lives easier. How many other great ideas might we fail to hear if we don't give *everyone* equal footing?

WHAT ARE THE NEXT STEPS ON YOUR JOURNEY TOWARD HEALTH EQUITY?

- Do you know how your organization is perceived in the communities you serve? Do you have mechanisms in place for gauging such perceptions?

- Does your organization have the equivalents to our BERGs? If so, do they reflect the specific interests of your patient populations?

- Does your organization have the equivalents to our leadership councils that maintain a specific focus on diversity and inclusion?

- What mechanisms do you have in place for recruiting and retaining a workforce that reflects the communities you serve? What measures has your organization taken to ensure that it recruits the best possible talent?

- What measures do you have in place for sharing the successes and accomplishments of your employees with the larger community?

- Which of the strategies we have outlined for fostering an inclusive workforce do you already have in place?

PART III

INCLUSION AND ALLYSHIP

Part III builds upon the concept that by having an internal structural framework in place to coordinate the efforts for achieving diversity in an organization, the necessary change agents need to be in place to focus on shifting the culture and advancing the organizational mission. That emergent culture must be one that supports inclusion such that all stakeholders are treated with dignity and respect so that they share in the mission and vision and be empowered to become allies in the journey toward achieving health equity.

CHAPTER ELEVEN

CREATING AND SUSTAINING A CULTURE OF INCLUSION

We all should know that diversity makes for a rich tapestry,
and we must understand that all the threads of the tapestry
are equal in value no matter what their color.

—MAYA ANGELOU

No matter the quality and scope of the framework you create, the attempt to develop inclusive workplace cultures will be ongoing and constantly evolving. Even the best systematic framework, like our pillars approach, requires diligence. Change is, as discussed early in the book, difficult; moreover, creating an inclusive culture requires a substantive change to historical systems and asks that each individual turn to the best parts of their human qualities and away from some deep-set human instincts. Inclusion promises that people are able to be their authentic selves. In order to create and sustain a medical culture of inclusion, we have to see our patients first as people. In essence, the path toward genuine inclusion is for all medical professionals to ask themselves, "What if the patient in front of me was my mother or my grandfather, my child or my partner; how would I treat them at this moment when they so depend on me?" When we return to the humanism such questions inspire, we don't see inclusion as a political or sociological term but an entirely natural human trait. An inclusive culture is one where *every* individual is treated with dignity and respect. To attain inclusion, we must create systematized mechanisms for acknowledging and confronting unconscious bias. To attain inclusion will require the full application of all the pillars we have outlined *and* the promotion of change among individual behaviors.

We opened Northwell Health's tenth symposium on diversity, inclusion, and health equity as we do all Northwell events—with a story of a patient experience. That idea in itself, sharing narratives of our and our patients' experiences, is an act of inclusion, for the only way to walk in the shoes of others, which is something that is required if we are to reignite human connections, is to learn directly from their experiences. And when your mandate is to serve anyone who walks through your doors with excellent care, the stories they can share of your successes and your failures hold lessons for your organization.

The story shared at the symposium was that of SC, who told of her family's experience at Northwell during the first wave peak of COVID-19 in the spring of 2020. There are many lessons we can take away from her story. Among them is the reinforcement that the pathway to health equity is a lengthy one that is littered with stumbling blocks and hazards.

Before the first wave of COVID-19 in New York City waned, SC, her son, and her husband all suffered its grip, with her husband experiencing the worst symptoms of the family, severe enough that he was hospitalized for over forty days. Still in need of medical attention but over the most fearsome symptoms, her husband was transferred to a rehab wing hospital. There, still fighting several symptoms of the disease, bored, isolated, longing for home, her husband passed several sleepless nights. Exhausted but unable to sleep, he asked for medication that might help him, knowing that proper sleep would aid his recovery. A psychiatrist was summoned for a consult. The psychiatrist barely heard her husband's request before he curtly told him he would not grant him medication. SC's husband, a pastor with a large congregation, a chaplain for the Suffolk County Sheriff's Department, a former college professor, and a busy community activist, tried to explain that he needed intellectual stimulation, a way to occupy his mind and be active if he were to sleep without some medical intervention. "All the room could offer, all day long, was the drone of a television," he explained to the psychiatrist.

As her husband passed along his experience, his wife recalls how he described watching the doctor shut down, "like he had Venetian blinds over his eyes that started to close." Her husband asked for humanitarian compassion, saying, "I'm like you. I used to teach college. I own thousands of books. I need people to whom I can talk." SC reflects on her husband's experience: "This White man could not believe that a Black man" who looked unkempt and exhausted after more than three weeks in the hospital battling daily for breath could be an intellectual and man of the cloth. The psychiatrist, after a consult that lasted minutes, recommended that her husband be placed in the dementia ward. Only after reaching out to other doctors with whom she had a personal relationship was SC able to stop the transfer and have the psychiatrist's diagnosis stricken from her husband's medical record. Those personal relationships with other physicians had been formed because both she and her husband were well-known community activists; indeed, her husband had once been a board member at that very hospital.

Perhaps the most remarkable thing about SC's narrative is the lack of bitterness or affront with which she explains that clearly, her husband was the victim of the psychiatrist's implicit bias. Her husband had not been heard. He had been dismissed because he did not, as she put it, "fit one's mental concept of who we should be or what we should look like." Appreciative of Northwell Health reaching out to her to share her story so that we might learn from it, she explains that she now routinely asks medical professionals who recommend treatment for herself or her family members: "What would you do if this was your mother? What would you do if this was your husband or your father or your son?" Her questions offer those in charge of her family's care a humanistic frame for contextualizing their relationship and a reminder that not only is a patient a person, but every person also deserves to be heard.

The lesson that SC wishes Northwell Health leaders and employees to take from her family's story is that people be seen as

Inclusion promises that individuals are allowed
to be their authentic selves.

unique individuals and not victims of a disease or assumptions based on their biology. Inclusion promises that individuals are allowed to be their authentic selves. An inclusive environment is one where *every* individual is treated with dignity and respect. In organizational settings, inclusion is the practice of providing equal access to opportunities and resources for people who might otherwise be excluded or marginalized. Perhaps the key language in this definition is "equal access to opportunities and resources." Inclusion isn't about asking to be treated differently; it's being treated by recognizing who you are and being presented with the opportunities to be all you wish to become. As Dr. Richard Carmona, the former US surgeon general, said at the same symposium where SC shared her story, inclusion offers individuals "the opportunity to thrive" rather than be forced to expend all their energy trying to survive. Author, lawyer, consultant, and vice president of Inclusion Strategy at Netflix, Vernā Myers, may explain inclusion even more succinctly when she says, "Diversity is being invited to the party. Inclusion is being asked to dance."[63] We see inclusion as creating a sense of belonging. It's about creating a space where people can tell their stories. Looking backward across what we have already discussed, you readily see how the pillars we have developed, those like developing education on cultural competency or forming community partnerships, need one another. And none can work without inclusion.

Achieving equity, diversity, inclusion, and belonging is key to delivering on our mission, performance outcomes, and commitment to remaining a great place to work ... for all. It defines our character and identity as an organization, and in its absence, we cannot truly claim victory in serving our diverse communities and attracting and retaining a diverse and talented workforce.

—JOSEPH MOSCOLA, PA
Executive Vice President, Enterprise Services, Northwell Health

THE EVERYWHERE ORDINARINESS OF UNCONSCIOUS BIAS

In SC's story, she rightfully labels the psychiatrist's dismissive treatment of her husband as the actions of one holding implicit bias. While we will utilize the term unconscious bias throughout this book, as we do in the many training sessions we hold for our employees every year, SC has properly recognized that by making false assumptions about her husband because of his race and his appearance, his doctor cast judgment that had a direct impact on his diagnosis and treatment. This story reveals not just the inhumane viewpoints people can hold but how those perspectives can directly alter patient outcomes. Had SC not intervened on her husband's behalf, how might the course of his treatment, and his life, been altered had the diagnosis of dementia been retained in his medical record?

Her story demonstrates what lies at the heart of unconscious bias: people make assumptions. We're all guilty of doing so. Sometimes they arise from our personal experiences. Some are passed on to us in childhood; nearly all are present in us out of a lack of meaningful exposure to those we believe to be different from ourselves. Think about your own reactions to others. If you encounter someone who does not appear to speak English, do you assume they have lower intelligence than your own? How likely are you to assume that non-English speaker doesn't have insurance? If you are working with an elderly patient who seems to have difficulty describing their symptoms, do you assume they have dementia? If you have a woman presenting with cardiac heart disease symptoms, are you more likely to assume the symptoms are due to stress or anxiety than if your patient were a man? Sadly, these scenarios are only too common, and there's evidence to show that such assumptions have an impact on care. There is a growing body of research that reveals stark disparities in diagnosis and treatment among women and racial minorities and their male and White peers. For example, a study by the University of Leeds in the UK found that women had a 50 percent higher chance than men of receiving the wrong initial diagnosis following a heart attack.[64] A 2015 study revealed that Black Americans are systematically undertreated for pain relative to White Americans and that a substantial portion of those seeking medical educations hold and may use false beliefs about biological differences between Blacks and Whites to inform medical judgments.[65] These are but two examples representative of the outcomes that can result from applying unconscious bias. But they are the example that proves illustrative of a larger phenomenon.

In medical settings, unconscious bias certainly is not restricted to providers. It flows both ways, and just as we can document its presence in how clinicians perceive their patients, patients unconsciously cast judgment about their providers. This is true based on gender and race, just as it is true that patients assume that a clinician who is heavy provides different medical advice than one who is slim. It is so common among female physicians of color to be mistaken by patients for nurses, custodians, or technicians that most nearly come to expect such behavior as a rite of passage. Receiving inappropriate comments is nearly as regular. The origin of such patient behavior is an unexamined notion about "what a doctor is supposed to look like."

The irony, of course, is that many such patients, like their clinician counterparts, don't view themselves as racist, sexist, ageist, or homophobic. Unconscious bias operates outside of the person's awareness and can be in direct contradiction to a person's espoused beliefs and values. What is so dangerous about unconscious bias is that it automatically seeps into a person's affect or behavior and is outside of the full awareness of that person. The scientific evidence suggests that unconscious biases develop at an early age and emerge during middle childhood. As Jennifer Eberhardt, a MacArthur Foundation grant recipient, reminds us, "You don't have to be a bigot to be biased. You don't have to be a bad person. You can have these biases ... that can have real devastating impacts despite your intentions and despite your desires."[66]

Eberhardt, author of the book *Biased: Uncovering the Hidden Prejudice That Shapes What We See, Think, and Do*, also highlights something central to our approach at Northwell Health, that what is important in confronting our biases is being conscious of the circumstances that make us vulnerable to them and then work to mitigate those factors. Unconscious bias training is effective because it allows participants to realize that they don't have to see themselves as villains or monsters. Rather than giving in to a culture where such biases can feel everywhere present, we can learn to give voice to those that exist within us. That's the key starting point. As Eberhardt suggests, "Understanding the situations that make us more or less vulnerable to bias, that's key. Even though we're vulnerable, we're not always acting on it. We don't have to be held in its grip. Understanding what those situations are that allow us to behave in ways that are free of bias or to make decisions in ways that are free of bias; that's a good thing."⁶⁷ In healthcare settings, we can foster such understanding by putting our team members in the shoes of the patients and help them to empathize with what patients are experiencing. This is another reason sharing stories can be so important. Empathy often starts by reminding people why they got into healthcare in the first place. And it is augmented by reminding them that both parties are human. When we individualize relationships, everything shifts. When we remember that the cancer patient seated before us is scared, our ears open. When we realize that their fear is not just of the disease or of death but because they are a parent who does not want to lose their child or cause fear in those they love, we begin to see the life realities that must be a factor in treating their disease. That fundamental ability to respect what another is experiencing is as important to potential recovery as our medical interventions.

The Center for Equity of Care develops educational offerings that get team members talking during and after unconscious bias training. The more they can share about themselves and be honest about their reactions to patients, the sooner they can begin to face the biases they hold. Admitting bias is a step toward creating empathy. Promoting empathy, which we define as the cognitive and emotional capacity to understand or feel another person's experience from within that person's frame of reference, has long been established as an essential strategy for dismantling racism. This is yet another reason that education must be a pillar in the construction of a systematic framework for diversity and inclusion.

Empathy often starts by reminding people why they got into healthcare in the first place.

We've even begun to experiment with new mechanisms for promoting empathy. One such experiment is a study in which participants experienced a sixty-minute, interactive, large-group session on microaggressions and, as individuals, a twenty-minute virtual reality (VR) module.[68] These were followed by group reflection and debriefing. The VR module used the film *1000 Cut Journey*,[69] which was developed at research labs at Columbia and Stanford Universities and premiered at the Tribeca Film Festival in 2018. Using VR technology to engage the film,

> *participants experience racism from the viewpoint of Michael Sterling, a Black male, at three different time points in his life: at age seven, sitting on the floor playing with blocks and being unfairly disciplined by a teacher and taunted by children; at age fifteen, kneeling on the ground while experiencing an intense interaction with aggressive police; at age thirty, being ignored and dismissed during a professional interaction surrounding a job interview, and then sharing a big moment with a romantic partner while listening to a voicemail from the interviewer explaining, "You aren't a good cultural fit for the organization."*[70]

While VR modules like this one aren't yet the norm for training, at Northwell Health, every employee, from senior leaders to the most recent hire, undergoes unconscious bias training. What all training shares in common is a core element of humanism: a return of the human touch by having participants see interactions beyond the limitations of their own experience. Whether that's more literal by experiencing the world as Michael Sterling or through having frank discussions with coworkers in a guided, supportive environment, people expand their viewpoints by trying on other skins, so to speak, such that they are forced to look beyond their own experiences and perspectives. Our experience has been that people *want* to talk about these issues. They ask questions of one another. They solicit advice. They share solutions. They talk to colleagues and realize that not only are their individual experiences valid, but they also aren't anomalies. Everyone has acted on unconscious bias, and everyone has been its victim. By accepting this reality of being human, they fill their empathy tanks and approach patients with new enthusiasm and a desire to build trust.

By educating employees on unconscious bias, not only do we provide them a safe space for recognizing the assumptions they make as individuals, but we also provide them the tools to be able to problem solve. We instill in them an ability to hit pause and ask themselves if they are acting on bias. Just as we must face the assumptions we may make based on the language someone speaks or their sexual identification or the color of their skin, we also need to stop making assumptions about their ability to be an active participant in their care. We can't assume all our patients can read discharge instructions if they are not written in a health-literate manner, nor that they have access to technology and the apps developed to guide postoperative care. We can't assume that they have reliable transportation to attend their next appointment, that they have ready access to a pharmacy, or that they have the financial means to pay for either. Nor can we make the assumption that any of these listed possibilities are more likely to be true because of how they are dressed or because their address on their patient record suggests assumptions about the neighborhood in which they live. Inclusion means seeing our patient as one person, not a collective of other people. It means providing care and communication specific to the needs of that one person who is actually seated before us in an examination room or emergency bay.

ENHANCING INCLUSION

We believe education is key and that inclusion needs to be infused in everything we do within healthcare. To that end, the Center for Equity of Care has set about systematically developing educational platforms that enhance inclusion, such as highlighting the link of unconscious bias and its effect on healthcare delivery.

Similarly, we utilize our Inclusion Academy, an online platform for learning programs and resources for diversity, inclusion and health equity. This leadership platform is designed to provide coordinators, frontline managers, and directors with the tools necessary to implement and manage diversity and inclusion strategies at their local sites and facilities. Inclusion Academy is a one-stop shop for all things equity, diversity, and inclusion at Northwell Health. This asset will continue to grow to ensure our workforce is culturally responsive to the medical and patient experience needs of our patients, as well as help us in fostering and sustaining a culture of inclusion for all of our team members. The academy includes representation from the Collaborative Care Council, High Potential and Physician High Potential programs, Patient Experience Committee leaders, IT management, and human resource managers.

Additionally, we hold annual executive conferences and summits to provide our leadership with diversity, inclusion, and health literacy organizational strategies that promote patient outcomes and raise cultural awareness in the care of our patients and the communities we serve. We have partnered with Hofstra University to form the Medical Scholars Program, designed to increase diversity within the healthcare workforce by exposing interested students from underserved backgrounds to various healthcare professions by leading them through a rigorous five-week academic course. In 2019 we implemented "Be More," a virtual unconscious bias training at all emergency departments, just one of many targeted service area trainings we have developed over the last ten years.

We've also pioneered curricula for health literacy education and effective patient communication. In order to provide all patients with the ability to obtain, process, and understand basic health information and services needed to make appropriate health decisions, we established various interdisciplinary system-wide intramural education initiatives for health system employees. These have taken various forms, including online modules, courses at the Center for Learning and Innovation, patient safety rounds, classes through the Institute of Nursing orientation, lunch and learns, webinars, presentations at department meetings, monthly education tips, and community outreach programs, among others. Cementing the role of inclusion throughout our system, we've introduced the practice of sharing patient stories specific to both failures and successes related to creating a culture of inclusion as part of the Ground Rounds tradition. That we present examples of inclusion practices as part of this vital patient review process reflects how central this aspect of patient care has become. Expanding our discussion to include things like inclusive practices and the presence of unconscious bias alongside other patient medical experiences offers evidence that we are delivering on a twenty-first-century approach to care. The comprehensive nature of our larger approaches to

Expanding our discussion to include things like inclusive practices and the presence of unconscious bias alongside other patient medical experiences offers evidence that we are delivering on a twenty-first-century approach to care.

education is not only an effort to maximize the reach of the education we provide but a reinforcement of our belief that inclusion must be incorporated in every aspect of the patient experience.

Our multipronged approaches to education underscore something elemental to changing the culture of healthcare because they recognize that the forces that create disparity in treatment are omnipresent. We have to be diligent in not allowing the surrounding culture that has a history steeped in the mistreatment of groups regarded as different from the majority to be present in the places where we practice health-care; for humanism, like the Hippocratic Oath, dictates that we care for everyone who enters our facilities with the very best care possible.

These are some of the approaches we've taken to educate our colleagues about the importance of inclusion. Your own initiatives will necessarily look different because the communities you serve, and the makeup of your organization is distinct. But perhaps our approaches can serve as models to build from and can solidify an understanding of why such education is so crucial to the health of your work culture and to the health of your patients. Ours have all been rooted in the central concept of this book: creating mechanisms for humans to connect to humans. We can't forge such connections if we've built walls—invisible or otherwise—between one another. Inclusion is like cooking a delicious gumbo or composing a great mash-up—the more unique ingredients and the greater the presence of diverse cultural traditions, the better.

WHAT ARE THE NEXT STEPS ON YOUR JOURNEY TOWARD HEALTH EQUITY?

- Use the power of storytelling, and share a story from within your organization where the presence of unconscious bias altered a patient outcome.

- Share a story from within your organization where the recognition of the presence of unconscious bias offered an opening for a new and different conversation that fosters a more inclusive culture.

- What education programs do you already have in place to help foster an inclusive environment and to train your team members to face their own unconscious biases?

- How do you measure the effectiveness of your educational outreach on inclusion?

- Do you have a methodology in place for your patients to share their experiences, positive and negative, on whether they were made to feel heard and respected during encounters with your organization?

CHAPTER TWELVE

THE IMPORTANCE OF ALLYSHIP IN THE EVOLVING HEALTHCARE LANDSCAPE

*I raise up my voice—not so I can shout but so
that those without a voice can be heard.*

—MALALA YOUSAFZAI

Success in creating a diverse, inclusive workplace culture that meets the needs of twenty-first-century healthcare requires an omnipresence of partnerships—formal and informal. Allies are essential to ensuring diversity and inclusion goals, even if the strongest framework is in place. A central job for those charged with improving diversity and inclusion within health institutions is to illustrate that the task of such improvement is one shared by literally everyone. Every employee in your health organization has a role to play. Every employee must see that creating a culture where they and their patients feel valued and respected has a direct connection to improving patient health. Allyship is what connects all the pillars of the systematic framework we have developed, and it is the sense of shared mission that allyship represents that will allow health organizations to forge the most impactful, effective partnership of all: the one with the patient.

We have built a great foundation for a framework that moves Northwell Health closer to achieving equitable treatment for all of our patients, and yet attempting to attain a fully inclusive culture can feel like a Sisyphean task some days. But we—both at Northwell Health and as a broader culture—are making real progress. We're pushing the rock up the hill. Sometimes that hill feels like Mount Everest, but you still climb it one step at a time. That's a whole lot easier task when there's an army of allies available to help. We need partners. We need networks and collaborators. We need engaged, committed leaders. We need those seasoned veterans who have a knowledge of institutional history as well as those with fresh ideas. And just as we are fighting for diversity in the makeup of those who provide our healthcare, we need diversity of perspective. We can't make progress if we only listen to ourselves. Change is possible when you develop an intentional strategy, but we can't accomplish it alone.

We've added one more critical element to our pillars graphic above—the linking presence of allyship. Any pillar standing alone has limited strength or stability. However, as any engineer will tell us, once we have multiple pillars and we place them "under load" by creating a horizontal structure that connects them, they have tremendous resiliency, strength, and capacity. In engineering, this is the essential principle for how you "distribute load," and from it, you can build the tallest skyscrapers and the mightiest bridges. The same is true in the organizational systems and human service frameworks we built. By linking our pillars together, we create a systematic, interactive framework of tremendous strength and durability that is sustainable. As you see from the graphic, that linking force is allyship.

To help define allyship, we call attention to another aspect of our graphic, the listing of our strategic partners. At Northwell Health, that list includes Katz Institute for Women's Health, Center for Learning and Innovation, Feinstein Institutes for Medical Research, Patient Experience, Clinical Service Lines, Health Solutions, Community Relations, Human Relations, Schools of Medicine and Nursing, Procurement, Quality, Feinstein Institute for Medical Research, Office of the Chief Information Officer, Institute for Nursing, Graduate Medical Education, Community Investment, Ambulatory and In-Patient Sites. These organizational strategic partners are what allyship is all about. Indeed, the term "strategic partners" is not strong enough language to convey how critical they are to our mission to promote diversity, inclusion, and belonging throughout the Northwell Health system. They have fully embraced and act upon our mission and vision. They have integrated that mission for changing our patient experiences into their very DNA. We cannot accomplish our objectives without such allies in every nook and cranny of the larger organization. Nor can you. You must identify your allies and be intentional about forging relationships with them. That starts by helping them see how their objectives align with promoting diversity and inclusion.

But just as allyship must flow throughout an entire organization by promoting common values and objectives, it must extend beyond the organization and into the community as well. This is inherently, even overtly apparent in our pillars for developing community partnerships and expanding supplier diversity.

We view allies as those—inside and outside our organization—who actively promote and aspire to advance the culture of inclusion through intentional, positive, and conscious efforts that benefit people as a whole. To put it in the simplest terms, when we speak of allies, what we are really recognizing is that we're all in this together. When we say "all," we mean it. Allyship is about making certain that no one gets left behind. Striving to achieve fair treatment for every patient treated in a Northwell Health facility

When we say "all," we mean it. Allyship is about making certain that no one gets left behind.

demands participation from everyone who impacts that patient's experience—custodians and physicians, clerks and nurses, dining service employees and therapists. But it also means that all of our employees have a commitment to go beyond the walls of our facilities to advance social justice and equal treatment for everyone by ensuring that we all have access to the best healthcare possible.

We live our mission and our values, and through allyship, seek to build relationships with those in vulnerable populations based on trust, consistency and accountability through listening, supporting, and advocating on their behalf.

—MICHAEL DOWLING
President and CEO, Northwell Health

ALLYSHIP: MICRO AND MACRO

Our outreach with stakeholders throughout the Northwell Health system and beyond demonstrates our awareness that allyship must occur at the micro *and* the macro levels. Alliances are formed with the colleague down the hall *and* with the corporation or institution down the street and across the globe. Allyship is demonstrated in the actions of individuals and in the actions of organizational divisions and indeed within the organization as a whole.

Of course, we cannot forget the simple reality that organizations are made up of individuals. In this regard, it is worth recognizing that many aspects of allyship must be developed in and acted on by individuals. Yet we can't only task those who are the victims of inequality to carry the load. This point was echoed by a 2020 Presidential Advisory Statement issued by the American Heart Association:

> *The task of dismantling racism must belong to all of society. It cannot be accomplished by affected individuals alone. The path forward requires our commitment to transforming the conditions of historically marginalized communities, improving the quality of housing and neighborhood environments of these populations, advocating for policies that eliminate inequities in access to economic opportunities, quality education, and healthcare, and enhancing allyship among racial and ethnic groups.*[71]

Allyship, as defined by the Anti-Oppression Network, "is the practice whereby a person or group in a privileged position or position of power seeks to operate in solidarity with a marginalized person or group."[72] Allies recognize the existence of systemic health inequity and are empowered to advocate for change. Dr. Camara Jones, a family physician and epidemiologist, frames the need for allyship this way: "All of us need to recognize that racism exists, that it's a system, that it saps the strength of the whole society through the waste of human resources, and that we can do something about it. White people, in particular, have to recognize that acknowledging their privilege is important—that your very being gives you the benefit of the doubt."[73]

Following these micro-level applications of allyship means that a White or male or heterosexual ally will speak up if they witness behavior or speech that is degrading or offensive toward colleagues, patients, or vendors, and they will advocate for more women, people of color, members of the LGBTQIA+ community, and members of other underrepresented groups as keynote speakers and panelists. An ally will always give credit to the person who originally proposes an idea rather than taking the credit for his or her own role. They will believe others' experiences rather than assuming something couldn't happen because they haven't personally experienced it. At its core, allyship at the micro level is always about creating a climate where those with power use the stability of that position to make certain those who have not historically had power are seen, heard, and respected. Ultimately, allyship is about distributing power. An ally, literarily and figuratively, makes certain that everyone has a seat at the table, whether that table is in a boardroom, a conference room, a patient examination room, or a breakroom.

Allyship starts with speaking up, but calling out inequity is not enough. Even education regarding cultural awareness or unconscious bias is not enough. The next step is to initiate policies and procedures that act upon spoken demands for reform. Developing and providing leadership and oversight for such policy is the central work of any office focused on diversity and inclusion.

Creating a culture that supports diversity in its people results in a greater diversity of ideas, which cannot be accomplished without nurturing a culture of openness and acceptance. The building blocks of allyship are formed in education programs like the workplace harassment training we regularly conduct, and they are hardened through the targeted community and employee outreach efforts of many of our BERGs. Fostering allyship is guided by introducing sound change management practices. It is modeled by the behaviors and actions of leadership throughout a health organization. It's solidified by a relentless focus by everyone throughout the health organization staying focused on improving patient experiences and outcomes. Even individual actions based on big ideas aligned with patient care move allyship into the mainstream of our thinking, as evidenced by Buddy Mayer and his invention of the Hand Shield. Buddy's invention demonstrates a tangible example of how big a difference the actions of one individual can make. Buddy is also a great embodiment of a micro-level vision for wanting to improve patient and employee health by being attuned to the work environment. His example offers us a rich metaphor as well, for the Hand Shield offered a sensible preventative measure against the potential spread of viruses and bacteria. In a similar fashion, by perpetuating allyship throughout an organization, you offer a preventative measure against the contagion of inequity.

Working in consort with micro-level approaches, at the macro level, we must look for global approaches that can make inclusion grow exponentially. For example, a health organization with academic ties will demand that courses on diversity and inclusion will be part of the educational curriculum for doctors and nurses. This is part of why the list of strategic partners on our pillars graphic is so extensive. Every one of these partners takes an active, actionable role in giving all of our patients equal footing and equal voice. When we look within the alliances formed inside Northwell Health, we see a reminder about the interactive nature of the pillars, for it is impossible to achieve allyship among the diverse divisions of a huge health system without leadership that makes diversity and inclusion a

By perpetuating allyship throughout an organization, you offer a preventative measure against the contagion of inequity.

strategic priority and then provides the resources to accomplish that strategy. Similarly, it is impossible to provide the kind of education required to create a culturally sensitive, health-literate organizational environment without having outstanding change management practices in place. And as we have said throughout the book, in order to implement allyship with any stakeholder in your organization, you must be able to provide the data necessary to demonstrate both the needs and the business benefits within the organization and the impact on patient health.

When we recognize the imperative behind treating the whole patient and acknowledge the importance of the social determinants of health, we quickly see that not only do we need an "all-hands-on-deck" approach within the health system, but we also see that health partners aren't just found in hospitals and clinics. They are present in community banks, job placement or training programs, local schools, and nonprofit organizations.

Quite specifically, macro-level allyship acts upon the recognition that inequity in healthcare is directly impacted by the variance in the daily lives and accessible opportunities patients experience. The purpose behind forming alliances with those in positions to impact a holistic understanding of health is a response to the assertions made clear in this statement from the World Health Organization Commission:

> Traditionally, society has looked to the health sector to deal with its concerns about health and disease. Certainly, maldistribution of health care—not delivering care to those who need it—is one of the social determinants of health. But the high burden of illness responsible for appalling premature loss of life arises in large part because of the conditions in which people are born, grow, live, work, and age. In their turn, poor and unequal living conditions, are the consequence of poor social policies and

programmes, unfair economic arrangements, and bad politics. Action on the social determinants of health must involve the whole of government, civil society and local communities, business, global fora, and international agencies.[74]

As their statement makes clear, because of failures in social and economic policies, those in power in public and private institutions too often have created or sustained inequitable social determinants of health. It is only through allyship as macro and micro levels that we can challenge such inequities. By having allyship unite the pillars or our framework, we create a robust, multifaceted, sustainable system for challenging inequity.

The movement between micro and macro allyship is fluid and bidirectional. It's a simple principle, really, for you cannot develop inclusive organizations without the participation of empowered allies throughout them. The best way to get buy-in on the importance of inclusion from individuals is to have system-wide diversity and inclusion policies and programs in place. What can seem like a chicken-and-egg proposition is really an opportunity, for both individual and global actions of inclusive allyship originate from humanism. It's relatively easy for individuals to recognize when they have been the victim of discriminatory treatment, but it takes our inherent humanism—the humanist trait of empathy that our parents most likely implored us to act upon as children—to recognize when our colleague or our neighbor is victimized in the same manner. It's harder still to recognize injustice when it is practiced by institutions, is historically systemic, or is advanced through policies. This is what Ibram X. Kendi is suggesting when he writes, "Americans have long been trained to see the deficiencies of people rather than policy. It's a pretty easy mistake to make: People are in our faces. Policies are distant. We are particularly poor at seeing the policies lurking behind the struggles of people."[75]

It is this linkage of individual people to policy that is at the center of allyship. Reigniting humanism means creating a seismic shift from seeing the *deficiencies* of individuals and people to seeing the *abilities* of individuals and people and then helping create opportunities for them to act on those abilities. Only then can we begin to implement policies that change institutions. Diversity and inclusion are the engine and the drivetrain that power you along your journey that has equity as its destination. Allyship is the fuel.

ALLYSHIP AMONG COMPETING HEALTH ORGANIZATIONS

One of the oddities in the healthcare industry is that, despite the humanist impulse to treat all who turn to a health organization for care, it is as competitive as any industry imaginable. In a place like metropolitan New York City and its Long Island suburbs, we have sizable, capable competitors literally around every corner. Northwell Health may be a nonprofit system, but that doesn't lessen the competition; indeed, it only enhances it because we have to provide state-of-the-art care on razor-thin margins. Like with all competitive enterprises, if we fail to provide superior, personalized service applying the most advanced practices of the industry, our patients will choose to go somewhere else.

The healthcare environment is simultaneously competitive and cooperative. We must act on both principles. Creating a genuinely inclusive culture that embraces diversity will provide you a competitive advantage. At the same time, despite the intense competition among peer health systems, in order to provide the best healthcare possible, we've got to be intentionally collaborative with one another. Because we are aligned in trying to improve both individual and community health, we are inherent allies with our competitors.

It's in this spirit of collaboration that you've heard us discuss best practices applied by three of our peer institutions: Kaiser Permanente, Henry Ford Health Systems, and the Mayo Clinic. There are other health systems that achieve excellence in developing diverse and inclusive practices, but these are the three from whom we have learned the most and with which we have most frequently collaborated. They are among the trailblazers with which we shared findings, collaborated on program development, and jointly brainstormed ideas. You'll need that too. You need to reach out to contacts you have within other health organizations, just as you should reach out to us and those from whom we learned.

More than just learn from the successes of other health organizations, we must partner with them and act on the recognition that we share common patient objectives. It is that spirit in which we have developed informal alliances in the tristate area, a kind of consortium of colleagues from different organizations who discuss things like new regulations that emerge regularly in areas like language access and diverse hiring practices. Because the field remains in its fledgling stages, regulations often emerge without guidelines for how to meet them. It is exceedingly helpful to navigate such uncertainty by being collaborative with other organizations. In the area of language access, these informal partnerships have been so successful that we have created a consortium modeled after what started as an informal group. Now that we have a consortium that all New York hospitals can join, we are able to tackle problems head on, share experiences, and brainstorm solutions. This has given us opportunities like identifying vendors from whom we can source supplies. For example, during the worst of COVID-19, all area hospitals were encountering problems among hearing-impaired patients who relied on lip-reading to communicate, something that is obviously impossible when providers are wearing traditional masks. Because we had channels to come together as a larger group, we were quickly able to identify a vendor that could supply clear masks, saving delays in remedying the problem. This example points to a larger advantage of cooperation between health organizations because working together and sharing experiences with different vendors provides a tremendous asset for achieving supplier diversity.

Not only must we draw on the wisdom of those who have passed before us, but what we are undertaking is so complex that we also need all the help we can get. Only then can we refine our own approaches and find innovative ones that best fit the needs of our specific communities.

ALLYSHIP AT WORK

Let us illustrate what we mean by both micro and macro allyship and their intersection with examples. Allies always have skin in the game. In the following three examples, allyship with those invested in education are all featured, but they also share a common end goal that is unique to the ally relationship. In these examples, the benefit is in human capital—training potential colleagues and future health-care workers. At the macro level, allyship typically means bringing a number of entities together to align toward a common cause that can prove transformative in creating inclusion. A great example of this is Northwell Health's participation with New Yorkers for Children (NYFC). Founded in 1996 by Nicholas Scoppetta, the former commissioner of the Administration for Children's Services (ACS), NYFC works in partnership with ACS to improve the lives of youth in foster care and to engage New Yorkers in that effort. NYFC's organizational goal is to support efforts to improve the well-being of youth participants through education, career development, the acquisition of life skills, and strengthening the child welfare system. Specific to

Northwell Health's participation, we developed a pilot program in allyship with NYFC focused on training kids aging out of foster care who were not college bound but who expressed interest in entering the healthcare industry. After conducting job fairs to demonstrate the variety of careers available in healthcare, we helped develop job training programs and then hired some of the graduates of those programs and paired them with volunteer mentors.

One more program in the same vein is Northwell Health's Spark! Challenge. The Spark! Challenge is an annual program for high school students across the New York area that brings together educators, schools, and many passionate Northwell Health team members. Students who participate have the opportunity to learn about careers directly from our team members, igniting their spark for healthcare careers. The Spark! Challenge plays a vital role in helping reach, engage, and inspire tomorrow's healthcare leaders. In 2019 alone, among hundreds of Spark! projects, the winning team learned about an electroencephalogram (EEG) and how the placement of sensors on the head produces outputs, and in the process of their learning, they met patients who had experienced head trauma, including one patient who had a 3-D printed skull. The students then visited the morgue to learn about the brain postmortem. Another team had to learn and decide how to care for patients in a family practice facility, their peers had to form a capital cost estimate for a physician practice based on an outline of a practice assessment, and one team, in a project most directly related to our own passion, met with nonclinical healthcare professionals to discover career pathways in diversity and inclusion.

Our allyship with the Spark! Challenge and NYFC probably have you recalling our community health worker's story and her fruitful participation in the From the Community for the Community project. It is another example of how education and community partnership can change lives and add to a vibrant workforce. Her story also illustrates the microlevel role of allyship in action. It was her fellow employees at Northwell Health who, face to face, human to human, refused to accept that a colleague should struggle with homelessness and, using their connections within our organization and their knowledge of its resources, became her advocate. But equally important is to emphasize the role that she had in her clients' lives. Once empowered through her position as a community health worker, she dedicated her professional life to becoming the voice of the clients she served and ensuring that they had access to and education about their health. For those community members, she became the human face of allyship.

When you look at your own communities, and you inventory the programs and initiatives that already exist to serve people through the combined strength of businesses, institutions, and nonprofit groups, we are certain that you can see opportunities to extend your outreach through forging allyship. Your needs will be different from ours because your patients are different than ours. But the same kinds of alliances we have formed can enrich your patient's lives, improve their health, and strengthen their bonds with others. To succeed, allyship has to have a human face—like the collected faces of the mosaic we shared at the beginning of this book—that demonstrates how acting on compassion and empathy can change all of our lives for the good. It is a human face that offers reassurance we are all in this together.

WHAT ARE THE NEXT STEPS ON YOUR JOURNEY TOWARD HEALTH EQUITY?

- The informal can matter as much as the formal. Have you established reinforcing practices that allow your employees to come to know one another by more than names or titles or roles?

- Do you include patient stories in all presentations?

- What are organizations within your service area that help educate the healthcare workers of tomorrow? Have you formed alliances with them or with the institutions that partner with them?

- What are organizations within your service area that advocate for or provide services to those that represent marginalized groups? Have you formed alliances with them or with the institutions that partner with them?

- Has your healthcare system developed formal guidelines that provide your workforce with mechanisms for how those in positions of authority can champion others?

- Has your healthcare system developed educational materials that can assist employees in learning about allyship and ways that they can support their colleagues?

CHAPTER THIRTEEN

A PATH FORWARD

Not everything that is faced can be changed, but
nothing can be changed until it is faced.

—JAMES BALDWIN

Derek Feely, a senior fellow at the Institute for Healthcare Improvement, reminds us that in healthcare, "there can be no quality without equity." When the quality of care for any one patient is lowered simply because of their preferred language, the color of their skin, their gender or sexual orientation, or the socioeconomic patterns present in their zip code, the entire health organization has failed them, and the larger system is also harmed.

For the health organization, this harm can be reputational, and it can be financial. But it can also be demoralizing for patients and staff alike. And, of course, for the patient, when the quality of care is reduced, their health suffers, their outcomes are altered, and any negative perceptions they harbor are cemented in ways that have lasting consequences that are passed along to others. To ensure that every measure is taken so that no patient suffers such indignity or discrimination requires not just a concerted effort by all within the health organization but also a systematic framework built for the purpose. The needs of your own health organization will be distinct from our own because of the unique nature and circumstances of the population you serve. However, because our approach is comprehensive and has been constructed around six pillars that apply in every healthcare environment, our essential framework can prove adaptable to your needs. Use our examples and our experience as a stepping stone for creative problem solving specific to your unique needs. By addressing the questions included at the end of chapters throughout this book and gathered at the conclusion of this chapter, we have provided the means for you to self-assess your health organization's strengths and needs, allowing you first steps in charting your own path forward.

At Northwell Health, our journey toward health equity began in 2010 when we formalized our approach to diversity, inclusion, and health literacy with a team dedicated to addressing health disparities. As the office evolved in the following years to become the Center for Equity of Care, we accelerated our mission of achieving the highest quality healthcare outcomes capable of meeting individual values while maintaining quality and implementing twenty-first-century strategies. Like other health systems, we've increasingly worked to establish partnerships to improve the health of the communities we serve, and we have expanded our healthcare delivery model to focus on prevention and improve outcomes for the epidemic of chronic disease that ravages the United States. As the Center for Equity of Care has grown and evolved, we've increasingly realized the need to develop an intentional path with health equity as its ultimate destination. Over the course of this book, we have shared with you our own approach to making sure no one gets left behind when it comes to their most valuable asset: their health.

At Northwell Health, just as we neared the ten-year mark of our own journey toward health equity, the persistent inequities we battle have now been unmasked throughout the healthcare sector to those outside our industry by a global syndemic. The disparate response by an embattled healthcare system to COVID-19 has demanded that the general public and the leaders they elect must acknowledge the presence of racism and bias and the impact both have on people's health. Inequities can no longer be ignored or wished away. One landmark report issued by the Institute of Medicine laid bare why this is true:

> Racial and ethnic minorities tend to receive a lower quality of healthcare than non-minorities, even when access-related factors, such as patients' insurance status and income, are controlled. The sources of these disparities are complex, are rooted in historic and contemporary inequities, and involve many participants at several levels, including health systems, their administrative and bureaucratic processes, utilization managers, healthcare professionals, and patients.[76]

A 2001 book produced by an Institute of Medicine committee tasked with creating recommendations for raising quality standards through twenty-first-century care approaches laid the groundwork for the realizations above. The study committee focused part of its analysis on the clinical encounter itself and found evidence that stereotyping, biases, and uncertainty on the part of healthcare providers can all contribute to unequal treatment. The conditions in which many clinical encounters take place—characterized by high time pressure, cognitive complexity, and pressures for cost-containment—may enhance the likelihood that these processes will result in care poorly matched to minority patients' needs.[77]

Their analysis also concluded:

Minorities may experience a range of other barriers to accessing care, even when insured at the same level as whites, including barriers of language, geography, and cultural familiarity. Further, financial and institutional arrangements of health organizations, as well as the legal, regulatory, and policy environment in which they operate, may have disparate and negative effects on minorities' ability to attain quality care. A comprehensive, multi-level strategy is needed to eliminate these disparities. Broad sectors—including healthcare providers, their patients, payors, health plan purchasers, and society at large— should be made aware of the healthcare gap between racial and ethnic groups in the United States.[78]

As we come full circle in this book and think about the needs of the near future for those readers who are intent on either establishing or reinforcing health equitable systems of care in their own organizations, it's useful to return to what it is we are trying to achieve in the first place. Ultimately health equity means that every person has an opportunity to achieve optimal health regardless of race, ethnicity, level of education, sexual orientation, gender identity, employment status, neighborhood, or disability.[79] Historically, unequal health outcomes too often result when any one of these life conditions does not fit into a system better built to meet the needs of White, wealthy or middle class, educated patients from safe neighborhoods. It's also the frequent result when we establish health organizations that lower quality in order to accommodate overuse of their emergency services for routine care, face financial shortfalls due to heavy dependency or federal medical reimbursements, or struggle to properly staff health organizations for rural patients. Certainly, there is never an excuse for treating *any* patient with reduced quality care, whether they enter an emergency room during a flashpoint of multiple Level 1 traumas, communicate in a preferred language other than English, observe cultural traditions that are unfamiliar to the practitioner who tends to them, or require treatment at the peak of a pandemic. For too long financial resources, political clout, English fluency, and health literacy, among other factors, have created an unlevel playing field. Equity in care ensures that everyone has a fair and just opportunity to attain optimal health. To achieve equity for all, organizations across the healthcare continuum must work to build cross-sectional partnerships and work together to remove obstacles that adversely impact health outcomes. Factors such as socioeconomic status, access to healthcare, education, neighborhood, and physical environment, as well as the social and community context within which patients live, are part of a complex system of social determinants of health that play a significant role in creating long-standing disparities. The quality standards of twenty-first-century care require that health organizations apply an equity lens to identify and monitor disparities take responsibility for addressing those they find. The systematic framework we have built at Northwell Health's Center for Equity of Care develops an intentional, interconnected, patient-centered model for dismantling inequities. We have realized a great deal of success in changing our piece of the healthcare landscape, but we recognize that we have a long way to go. By making each of the pillars we have introduced in *Reigniting the Human Connection* more robust and more "cross-pollinated," we can expand on the building blocks we've spent the last ten years constructing.

A guiding principle for how we have conceived of our framework for accomplishing change is found in the foundational humanitarian position that you simply cannot achieve equity until you build health organizations that reflect and honor the diversity of the patient populations they serve and then cultivate a culture where those patients feel included as vital partners in achieving their desired health outcomes. When we build genuine relationships between diverse peoples, we take a first step to ensuring that every patient and every healthcare provider shares in decision making. We have spoken about a lot of different kinds of partnerships over the course of this text, but the most important one is between an individual and their health. To achieve that, there can't be barriers that make the options for health decisions clearer or more informed for one individual over another. All other partnerships, internal and external to the health system, operate in the service of this one. And all must acknowledge that only a fraction of what it means for an individual to be "healthy" can be addressed directly by healthcare organizations. Only 20 percent of any individual's health and well-being can be addressed by what we traditionally think of as healthcare, as determined by the ease of access to clinical care and the quality of care received. Overemphasis on clinical care discounts the significantly greater impact of an individual's health behaviors, their physical environment, and their socioeconomic factors. Any attempt to create an equitable health system must acknowledge this 80 percent of daily living and interact with patients from this holistic vision of their total health.

You can't complete this vital work alone, no matter how good your model is. Improvement advances must begin with all healthcare constituencies—health professionals, federal and state policy makers, public and private purchasers of care, regulators, organization managers and governing boards, and consumers. All stakeholders must begin to committing to this fundamental principle as voiced in the National Prevention Strategy, accepting as their explicit purpose "to continually reduce the burden of illness, injury, and disability, and to improve the health and functioning of the people of the United States."[80] In order to act on this commitment, as the committee on the Quality of Health Care in America report makes clear, we must urgently redesign the American healthcare system and provide overarching principles for specific direction for policymakers, healthcare leaders, clinicians, regulators, purchasers, and others.

As you shift your culture to meet this commitment, you are wise to keep the following principles found in the Michigan Health and Hospital Association report "Eliminating Health Disparities to Advance Health Equity and Improve Quality" in mind:

- Develop a deeper understanding of the needs, perspectives, interests, values and beliefs of all patients and families from diverse backgrounds.

- Implement actions that reflect what matters most to patients at each level of hospital care.

- Evaluate whether the measures and metrics set forth are consistent and relative to different patient populations.

Our emphasis on the human connection in healthcare is echoed in the book *Crossing the Quality Chasm: A New Health System for the 21st Century*, written by the Committee on Quality of Health Care in America, Institute of Medicine. Part of what distinguished this text, now written twenty years ago, if the recognition that an essential measure of quality in healthcare had to be that it was equitable. Their report was groundbreaking by insisting that equitable care was as important to measuring quality as safety, effectiveness, the patient role, timeliness, and efficiency. Among the recommendations they issued that laid the foundation for their vision of twenty-first-century care were these:

- Customization based on patient needs and values. The system of care should be designed to meet the most common types of needs but have the capability to respond to individual patient choices and preferences.

- The patient as the source of control. Patients should be given the necessary information and the opportunity to exercise the degree of control they choose over healthcare decisions that affect them. The health system should be able to accommodate differences in patient preferences and encourage shared decision making.

- Anticipation of needs. The health system should anticipate patient needs rather than simply reacting to events.[81]

Whatever final health equity framework you adopt, such a problem-solving, patient-focused lens is required. These qualities have been cornerstones in our own approach and reflect our fundamental belief for why the human connection between patients and providers undergirds all of our policies, actions, and initiatives. Moreover, a twenty-first-century model of care will remind you that your hospitals, ambulatory practices, and other arms of your health organizations are not islands. They exist within the great sea of environments and social determinants of health where your patients spend their lives.

Creating a holistic view of health for patients *and* for their providers saves lives. In a patient as partner model, because patients are empowered, the rate of readmissions falls significantly due to far fewer incomplete treatment plans or unmonitored disease complications. As a result, this model not only delivers better patient outcomes, but it also reduces costs. We spend less time addressing recurrent medical problems, see fewer medical emergencies, require fewer tests, and have a significant step up in successfully managing chronic disease. Remove more medical complications, resolve treatable illnesses and conditions, avoid future medical emergencies, and patients and health organizations alike can preserve financial resources. National analysis has estimated that health disparities cause approximately $93 billion in excess medical care costs and $42 billion in lost productivity annually.[82] The economic burden of these health disparities in the United States is projected to increase to $126 billion in 2020 and $353 billion in 2050 if the disparities remain unchanged.[83] We should not be surprised that knowledge really is power, and knowledge in the hands of patients can help them make decisions that save health organizations money while providing better outcomes.

Moreover, without carefully nurtured community partnerships, healthcare systems do not have the means to alter the social determinants of health that may dominate the zip codes where their patients live. Social determinants of health are unique to every individual, of course, but health-outcome-focused programs developed in partnership with established community, governmental, and faith-based entities can target populations that share population patterns. That necessitates having the kinds of relationships and communication venues within your community to identify needs in the first place. Let's say, for example, that you know that the community you serve hosts a statistically high segment of smokers. An evidence-based, interactive, and supportive smoking cessation program developed by a healthcare system can exponentially increase its reach and effectiveness when it partners with an organization that is known and trusted in a community and has the active support of respected community leaders like faith-based organizers, school administrators, coaching associations, or large employers. As is the truth for nearly all health initiatives, even the most carefully constructed program cannot change the lifestyle choices of all its patients, but in a case like this example, every patient who does choose to stop smoking because of the intervention of their health organization will enjoy a direct health benefit while the health organization can free up resources and reduce costs for every patient who is further removed from health complications directly tied to smoking. Similarly, a health organization alone cannot resolve the complex health effects of substandard housing, but it cannot truly serve its patients if it ignores the problem, and it might be able to provide safe, affordable housing to a number of its employees.

Before you can implement creative, solution-minded programs, you have to understand your patient population. You can't do that if they feel excluded. In a system the size of Northwell Health, dominant patient needs vary wildly from one service location to another. While we may need to address food insecurity for many of our patient populations, you may serve an area where nutritious food is readily accessible, but physicians or advanced medical diagnostics technologies are not.

So where do you start? For Northwell Health, as we've detailed, our starting point was in addressing accurate data collection. Our experience supports the fact that you need meaningful benchmarks that offer concrete ways to determine whether disparities exist within your system.

A data-driven portrait of whom you serve is essential to identify the presence of disparities.

It's the old business mantra "You can't manage what you don't measure." Leaders should ask themselves: How do we know if we have disparities? If we do, how can we prevent disparities that exist in our patient outcomes? We can't solve disparities we have not identified. The benchmark survey we've referenced throughout the book was a critical first step for us. From it, we were able to identify the most pressing needs where change could produce the greatest impact. You need to inventory your organization on key metrics, including race, ethnicity, preferred language, and service area. A data-driven portrait of whom you serve is essential to identify the presence of disparities. Beyond inventorying such metrics about your patients, you must create mechanisms to hear from them, learn about their experiences within your health organization, and gain their perspective on how they view their interactions and how such interactions have affected their health outcomes.

Let us share two brief examples of the positive change that can come from applications of this kind of data.

The chief of the emergency department at one of our hospitals studied patterns of patient-identified preferred languages and self-disclosed emergency room employee language preferences and cultural backgrounds. This hospital is situated in one of the highest linguistic and ethnically diverse populations in our health system. She learned that 30–40 percent of emergency room and treat-and-release patients at her hospital self-identified as limited English proficiency (LEP) for their healthcare communication. Further, a review of data available from our system dashboard revealed that LEP patient visits to the emergency room lasted twenty-five minutes longer than English-speaking patients.

Based on data findings and interviews with a number of staff members, the ER chief created a staffing schedule that attempted to pair patients and ER staff based on culture and language. Her experiment quickly revealed that her department's interpretive services capacity was lacking tremendously. As a result, she ordered an additional seven video remote interpreting (VRI) devices and began including interpretation services as part of the department's daily rounding. An assembled frontline team created a vision statement to guide their efforts: "Safe and compassionate care through teamwork and positive communication." This mission statement was shared and discussed during daily huddles and staff meetings and in monthly newsletters. By the second month of implementation, these changes resulted in decreasing the department's door to treat time as well as treat-and-release time by fourteen minutes and ultimately saw that those patients who accepted interpreter services in triage experienced shorter treatment times than their English-preferred counterparts. She also examined patient satisfaction reports. Those reports revealed that patients who interacted with trained staff interpreters or through VRI devices in preferred languages other than English routinely rated their experience satisfaction higher than patients who used English as their preferred language. By gathering data and then taking action on what that data revealed, this ER chief realized quite the turnaround.

In another initiative involving emergency rooms, the Center for Health Equity developed a program focused on unconscious bias training. Recognizing not only that unconscious bias can affect clinician's decisions but that the unique context of emergency health medicine can create susceptibility to bias, we developed a program titled Breaking Bias in Healthcare. Between April and June 2019, fifty-one emergency medicine attending physicians from four hospitals in New York City and Long Island, along with six senior health systems leaders and four unconscious bias training program facilitators, participated in this self-paced, interactive, online learning program. The program was created to increase awareness of unconscious bias and its impact on patient care and health disparities and to teach strategies to reduce bias among health professionals. Aggregate self-reported scores on an Implicit Association Test indicated a reduction in race-based bias upon program completion, and 93 percent of participants agreed that unconscious bias can be reduced by practicing mindfulness strategies. By identifying a fixable problem and demonstrating the will to address it, we were able to help physicians become mindful of their beliefs and actions and initiate steps to remove this barrier to equitable care. The program revealed a powerful fact: you can't change what you don't face. Do you recall the example we used of a physician who diagnosed a Black COVID-19 patient with dementia simply because he could not accept that his patient was starved for intellectual stimulation while in isolation? Having fallen prey to common racial stereotypes, the physician failed to see the unique human being in front of him. How might have the application of twenty-first-century patient interaction practices or a simple unconscious bias training staved off the nearly tragic consequences should his patient have been moved to an Alzheimer's unit?

The two examples we've just provided of implemented change to meet patient needs both have the end result of moving practices closer to equitable outcomes. Both were dependent on getting to know patients as individuals, one by having patient data readily available, the other by teaching practitioners to be mindful of their own biases and meet the patient where they are at.

Once you identify a hierarchy of concerns that have the greatest impact on disparities for your patients, you must determine what will be the most effective contributing factors in creating a culture that reduces disparities. Accurate data is key. If you identify any groups of patients where the quality, outcomes, safety, or experience scores are lower than the rest, take an intentional look at these groups, why those disparities occur and what is missing in your system or culture. Reducing disparities means looking at your approaches to diversity and inclusion in a broad, stratified manner, including socioeconomic status, environment, and social determinants of health. Without such a comprehensive perspective, you can't identify gaps that can result in treatment disparities. Our own strategy was to build, pillar by pillar, the systematic framework that has been the central focus of much of this book. Every pillar was constructed from a foundation of reigniting human connections that already existed within our system but that needed to be enhanced and formalized. Our approach closely parallels another what is summarized effectively in the white paper "Achieving Health Equity: A Guide for Health Care Organizations" produced at the Institute for Healthcare Improvement. The paper opens with this vital reminder acknowledging the full scope of where disparities arise:

> *Significant disparities in life expectancy and other health outcomes persist across the United States. Health care has a significant role to play in achieving health equity. While health care organizations alone do not have the power to improve all of the multiple determinants of health for all of society, they do have the power to address disparities directly at the point of care, and to impact many of the determinants that create these disparities.*[84]

Through systematic efforts to remove disparities within our health system, and by creating cross-sectional partnerships with organizations and businesses in the communities we serve to help reduce the impact of other social determinants of health we can't alter alone, we have consistently removed barriers to access and have changed the relationship with our patients to a model where they know we are focused on their individual needs. Our model emphasizes a holistic approach to healthcare that treats the patient as a partner and sees individual patients as unique humans with unique lives and experiences, not as vessels of disease or chronicles of conditions. Only then can we develop alternatives to patterns of healthcare uniformity and exclusion that have kept individuals from realizing their best health. You will need to create mechanisms that allow you to more fully understand the demographics, environments, and social determinants of health that predominate your own patient population. The pillars we have constructed are architected with a twenty-first-century approach to patient care, one that starts by meeting patients where they are at—literally and metaphorically. Our ultimate aim doesn't apply to isolated individuals but to *every* individual. Meeting the needs of diverse individuals inside the scope and complexity of a modern health organization requires practical, pinpoint guidance for establishing policies, procedures, approaches, and best practices, just as it requires providing targeted resources and critical steps to support such endeavors. Care that is efficient, effective, safe, and timely cannot be patient centered or equitable if Mike or Mary is served in a manner that creates a different outcome than Miguel or Mariá.

Among the benchmarks that we strive to meet with our past and our future projects aimed at achieving health equity, we start by acknowledging the importance of incorporating an equity lens into all improvement strategies, including quality, patient safety, and population health. As we reach out to allies within our own health system, we focus on establishing a common understanding of the role of everyone and every unit within Northwell Health in addressing health disparities. As you implement new strategies within your own organization, you will quickly discover that partnering with others to achieve health equity goals also requires creating the means to assess the level of implementation of key aspects of our system-wide strategic plan; diversity and inclusion cannot be achieved if any gaps remain in the system, for it is human nature to remember the single moment when they felt unheard or ignored even if they viewed all of the rest of their encounters positively. Moreover, even a single incident can have a profound effect on whether a patient will take the actions to become a partner in their own care or recovery. Programs and interventions must target fundamental causes that lead to disparities in outcomes, moving beyond one-type-fits-all models.

The path forward will require not only improved and consistent application of the principles represented in each of our six pillars, but it also will need better cohesion between them. It requires robust strategies to accomplish such cohesion. For example, as a means to improve community health equity, Northwell Health established the Community and Population Health Department, bringing together the Center for Equity of Care and the departments of Community Health and Community Relations. The mission: to measurably improve the health and wellness of our communities by developing enduring community partnerships and working together to address community health needs.

As the workforce changes to better reflect the patient population any health organization serves, its leadership will also have to diversify.

Even a single incident can have a profound effect on whether a patient will take the actions to become a partner in their own care or recovery.

When we look at the long-term path ahead of us, it is one that must have equal representation of all marginalized populations at the highest leadership levels, for until women, people of color, LGBTQIA+, veterans, disabled people—all the voices from young to old, from native born to immigrant—are present in senior leadership, there will be inherent bias present.

Because the change we require is sweeping, we can't accomplish it alone. A multidisciplinary coalition composed of providers, trainees, and staff (clinical and administrative) who are dedicated to developing and executing strategic initiatives that focus on topics such as inclusive climate, patient care, and professional development is needed. This sort of coalition is foundational for achieving diversity and attaining an inclusive work culture with the objective of creating an environment where every member of our community is respected, valued, and heard. Elements that are essential to achieving community health equity include:

- developing a team that reflects the diversity of the populations we serve

- advancing the field through inclusive research and training

- broadening our community outreach

- promoting empathetic communication to ensure that all community members feel respected, valued, and heard

We not only need clear directives from healthcare leaders based on a humanist and deeply moral foundation, but we also need buy-in from every level of our health organizations and from the other entities that help shape healthcare policy. A new health system for the twenty-first century will demand both shifts in perspective and new infrastructure. We must face the reality of local and global environmental changes simultaneous to human-focused changes. Those that suffer the greatest impacts of global climate change have consistently been the poor, people of color, and those with the least access to quality healthcare. As historic patterns have shown, global climate change increases human migration out of devastated regions, creates more influx into populated urban areas, worsens food and potable water insecurity, stresses healthcare systems and governmental health administration programs, and generally widens existing economic divisions. Demographic models have routinely shown that the United States will continue to become more diverse. Growing economic and environmental pressures will expand the mosaic that is this nation. To meet the needs of all of its citizens require a multidisciplinary approach to problem solving. The twenty-first-century healthcare system in which we proudly participate provides care that is evidence based, patient centered, and system oriented. This, in turn, implies new roles and responsibilities for patients and their families, who must become more aware, more participative, and more demanding in a care system that should be meeting their needs. All involved must be united by the overarching purpose of reducing the burden of illness and disability in our nation.

Among our lasting commitment to achieve these aims, we at Northwell Health continue to focus on and grow our abilities to:

- link quality care to equitable care;

- increase collection and use of race, ethnicity, and language preference data and use the data to identify and solve for healthcare delivery disparities;

- educate and integrate the tenets of cultural humility into all aspects of the healthcare delivery model;

- increase cultural competency training with the ultimate aim of having every team member undergo initial training and then see ongoing training/focus as a routine part of their development;

- develop and sustain a culturally responsive approach to care;

- increase diversity in governance and all areas of leadership;

- improve and advance community partnerships; and

- eliminate components of institutional racism in the health system.

Applying the foundational pillars we have developed consistently and interactively offers us the mechanism to succeed with these stated aims. Of course, underlying all the pillars is our recognition that the surest path to eliminating disparity is found in embracing the full spectrum of diverse perspectives. The more eclectic and more vibrant the mosaic we are able to create among the human beings that make up any healthcare organization, the better we can care for all the individuals who entrust themselves to it.

IMPLEMENTATION FRAMEWORK FOR ADVANCING DIVERSITY, INCLUSION, AND HEALTH EQUITY

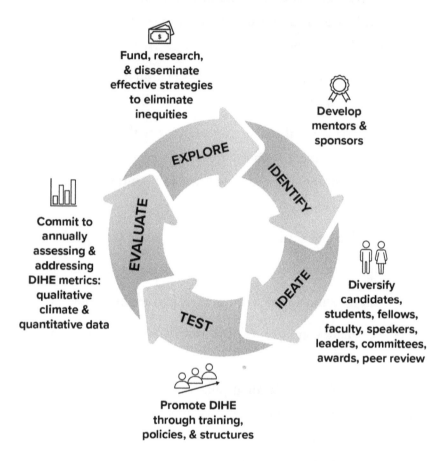

Source: Modified from R. B. Schnabel, E. J. Benjamin, "Diversity 4.0 in the Cardio-vascular Healthcare Workforce," Nature Reviews Cardiology 12, (2020), 751-753.

As you consider the pathway we have developed and the implementation framework illustrated above for embracing diversity and creating a climate of inclusion as it applies to your own health organization, we think it is valuable to reflect on this wisdom from Dr. George E. Thibault:

Each of us has our own touchstone for humanism—an experience, a role model, an inspirational writing. It is time for each of us to draw on that touchstone and make it more real in our daily lives. Let it inform every encounter with a patient, let it inform the work within each health system to make it more humanistic, and let it inform how each of us expresses our citizenship. Let us use our expertise and professional standing to speak out on issues that are important to our values and our patients.[85]

Thibault concludes with this observation: "It will be hard to have humanism in medicine if there is no humanism in the world around us. Human interest, values, and dignity must predominate."[86]

It was these essential humanist values that likely brought each of you, as it did us, to choose healthcare as a profession in the first place. If we are to succeed in achieving health equity for all, we'll be required to rekindle the human connections that make us commit our lives to the noble profession of healing.

> *The birds they sang*
> *At the break of day*
> *Start again*
> *I heard them say*
> *Don't dwell on what has passed away*
> *Or what is yet to be.*

—FROM "ANTHEM," BY LEONARD COHEN

ABOUT THE AUTHORS

JENNIFER H. MIERES, MD, is a Professor of Cardiology and Associate Dean of Faculty Affairs at the Zucker School of Medicine at Hofstra Northwell. As Senior Vice President of Northwell Health's Center for Equity of Care she has oversight of, and provides strategic guidance for, Northwell's diversity and health equity initiatives and serves as the health system's inaugural Chief Diversity and Inclusion Officer. Under Dr. Mieres's leadership Northwell Health has been recognized as a top health system for diversity, equity, and inclusion, most notably by Diversity Inc. as a "top ten" healthcare institution for a measurable commitment to healthcare justice. Northwell Health has been in the top ten list for nine consecutive years and was recognized as number one in 2020 and 2021.

A graduate of Bennington College and Boston University School of Medicine, she is a Fellow of The American Heart Association (AHA), American College of Cardiology (ACC), and Master of the American Society of Nuclear Cardiology (ASNC) and served as the first female President of the ASNC in 2009.

Dr. Mieres's clinical focus and research are centered on the elimination of health and gender disparities and cardiovascular disease in women. She is a leading advocate for patient-centered healthcare and medical education reform and has authored/coauthored over sixty-five scientific publications, including as lead author of the 2005 and 2014 AHA cardiac imaging guidelines for women. As an international speaker, she has presented her research as distinguished faculty at over a hundred forums and conferences, both nationally and internationally, including scientific sessions of the ACC, AHA, ASNC, the International Conference of Nuclear Cardiology, and IHI/BMJ International Forum on Quality & Safety in Healthcare.

A true patient and community advocate, Dr. Mieres is actively involved in service. She serves on the ACC's Diversity and Inclusion committee, is a national spokesperson for AHA's Go Red For Women movement, and has served as chair of several national AHA committees, as well as the Scientific Advisory Board for WomenHeart.

A prolific communicator, Dr. Mieres recently coauthored *Heart Smarter for Women: Six Weeks to a Healthier Heart* (Advantage Media Group, 2022). Her previous book, *Heart Smart for Women: Six S.T.E.P.S. in Six Weeks to Heart-Healthy Living* was published in October 2017 along with a Spanish version, *Un Corazón Saludable para La Mujer Moderna: Seis P.A.S.O.S. en Seis Semanas para Mantener la Salud del Corazón*, in February 2019. Following her Emmy-nominated documentary *A Woman's Heart* (2001), her creative ingenuity has evolved as an executive producer of a two-part documentary series *Rx: The Quiet Revolution* and *Rx: Doctors of Tomorrow* (2015). The films have forged a change in the healthcare narrative while garnering placement on national TV network PBS and in educational institutions. She is an executive producer of the women's health documentary *Ms. Diagnosed*, which premiered at the Cinequest film festival on March 7, 2020. Dr. Mieres is routinely called upon by national and local media for expert commentary and has been designated as a most-credible voice in the healthcare industry.

A recipient of several prestigious awards, Dr. Mieres has been recognized as a tireless force fostering diversity in medical education, gender equity in cardiovascular care, as well as eliminating disparities in the delivery of healthcare to the community.

Dr. Mieres resides in New York City with her husband, Dr. Haskel Fleishaker, and their daughter, Zoë Fleishaker.

CONNECT

@DrJMieres
www.drjennifermieres.com

ELIZABETH C. MCCULLOCH, PHD, is an Assistant Vice President for Diversity and Health Equity at Northwell Health. Dr. McCulloch established a system-wide language and communication access program, which has resulted in exponential growth of the use of interpretation services and health literacy strategies. As a leading healthcare strategist in the field of effective communication, she has developed innovative approaches, implemented comprehensive policies and procedures, and remained a passionate advocate for advancing health equity.

Dr. McCulloch routinely collaborates with multidisciplinary healthcare teams throughout the system to develop, coordinate, and implement standardized effective communication programs, practice delivery models, and performance metrics. As an Assistant Professor of Nursing at the Hofstra/Northwell Graduate School of Nursing, she is frequently called upon to deliver ongoing educational training programs for clinical and nonclinical staff and assesses competencies to ensure the delivery of culturally sensitive, quality care. With her background in statistical methodology and analysis, she has also codeveloped an interactive dashboard to explore health disparities and race, ethnicity, and language parameters. Dr. McCulloch has spent the last decade advocating for data standardization and data transparency with the goal of linking equity to quality.

Dr. McCulloch previously worked in the health system at North Shore University Hospital and The Krasnoff Quality Management Institute, where she supported Joint Commission disease specific certifications and contributed to the management of healthcare data, database creation, and analytical reporting.

Dr. McCulloch is recognized in the field of research and population aging. She is versed in research methodology and quantitative analysis and has had extensive experience in community health research. She has presented her work at numerous national and international conferences, including the IHI/BMJ International Forum on Quality and Safety in Healthcare and is widely published.

Dr. McCulloch holds a bachelor of science from Lafayette College in neuropsychology, a master of science from Hofstra University in gerontology, and a doctorate degree in social sciences from Fordham University. She has also served as a faculty member at Hofstra University and Columbia University. She is a member of several professional societies, including Phi Kappa Phi and Sigma Phi Omega.

Dr. McCulloch resides in Long Island, New York, with her husband, Dr. Kenneth McCulloch, and three sons, Jackson, Lucas, and Mason.

MICHAEL P. WRIGHT, EDD, served as Vice President of Diversity and Health Equity for Northwell Health. He joined Northwell Health in August 2014 and had oversight for ensuring the operational alignment and business success of equity, diversity, and inclusion initiatives across the health system. He partnered with clinical and administrative stakeholders to embed and sustain the tenets of diversity, inclusion, and health equity for team members, patients, and the communities served by the health system. While at Northwell Health, Dr. Wright established Northwell's Inclusion Academy and cosponsored the organization's Business Employee Resource Groups, amplifying the critical role they played in addressing community health needs and racism as a public health crisis.

Dr. Wright has twenty-five years of experience optimizing organizational talent strategies and enabling inclusive cultures. Over the span of his career, he has led diverse teams within eight industries across multiple domains of expertise including organizational change management, leadership and executive development, enterprise learning and development, talent management, diversity, equity, and inclusion. His roles have spanned global enterprises including Microsoft, Starbucks, Shaw Communications, Bank of Montreal, Exelon, Invensys Plc, and currently FM Global.

Throughout his career, Dr. Wright has had the privilege to learn from iconic leaders and has enjoyed successfully navigating various organizational cultures to drive business and team performance outcomes. Over the years, he has shared his passion for workplace learning, leadership development, and change by speaking at various national and international industry forums and conferences and has several publications.

Dr. Wright earned his doctorate degree from a joint program in business and workplace learning through the Wharton School of Business and the Graduate School of Education at the University of Pennsylvania.

Prior to his corporate career, he earned his bachelor of arts degree from the University of Waterloo – St. Jerome's College, where he spent several years preparing for priesthood in the Catholic Church in Canada. Following his undergraduate degree, he completed his master of divinity degree from the University of Toronto, St. Michael's College. In subsequent years, he earned a master of education in counseling psychology from the Ontario Institute for Studies in Education at the University of Toronto.

In 1995, Dr. Wright received the Order of St. John and a 10-year Service Medal from the Governor General of Canada for his leadership and passion for service in the community. Additionally, he served as Chair of the LENS Steering Committee for the National Center for Healthcare Leaders and has served on the Board of Directors for Leadership Tomorrow, a Puget Sound Region leadership development program and is a former member of the AIIR Consulting Advisory

Board. Dr. Wright currently serves as a strategic advisor for AIIR Consulting, a global leadership development consultancy, where he leads the strategy of AIIR Consulting's Elevate Project—a unique pro bono consulting initiative that serves nonprofit leaders around the world who are dedicated to solving some of the world's most intractable challenges including homelessness, education, and equity.

Dr. Wright is currently an assistant professor of organizational behavior at the Zarb School of Business, Hofstra University, Hempstead, New York and is a member of the Dean's Advisory Board for the School of Business. He previously served as adjunct faculty at the University of Maryland, College Park and has participated on doctoral committees for students graduating from the University of Pennsylvania Graduate School of Education program in business and workplace learning.

Dr. Wright resides in Providence, Rhode Island, with his partner, Peter, and their two dogs, Norman and Ritchie.

NEXT STEPS ON YOUR JOURNEY TOWARD HEALTH EQUITY

CHAPTER FIVE

WHAT ARE THE NEXT STEPS ON YOUR JOURNEY TOWARD HEALTH EQUITY?

- Use the power of storytelling, and share a story from within your organization that either illustrates the support you already have in place from a senior leader or one that demonstrates why the need for such support is evident.

- Is the driving force to address diversity and inclusion in your organization a mandate from your senior leadership which now needs to infiltrate the whole culture? Or is it a grassroots vision that needs to elevate the organization by recruiting senior managers to its cause?

- If the former, how can you place senior leaders in visible positions on diversity and inclusion opportunities that can demonstrate their commitment to the rest of the organization?

- If the latter, what aspects of humanism are central to individual leader's beliefs and experiences that you can draw on to engage them? Who are your best targets for cultivating leadership alliances? What appeals to your leaders regarding this work?

- What motivates your leaders to want to commit to this important work?

- Have you curated internal data and external research that helps you demonstrate both the need and the benefit from an organizational perspective and embrace diversity and inclusion? Where and with whom have you shared these materials? With whom do you share your insights, perspectives, trends, and analysis?

- What would you identify as the three most central attributes of your organization's core culture? Where do those attributes pose challenges for implementing your initiatives? Where do they present opportunities or suggest effective strategies for managing change? How do these attributes align with your vision for change?

WHAT ARE THE NEXT STEPS ON YOUR JOURNEY TOWARD HEALTH EQUITY?

- Share a story from within your organization when an instance of improving a patient's understanding of their condition and treatment plan resulted in them taking an active, responsible role in their own health journey.

- Have you conducted a survey to establish benchmarks for how well you provide health-literate interactions and materials so that your patients'/consumers' interests and experiences are measured? If so, what measure have you put in place to act upon its results?

- What measures do you have in place to really know who your patients are or where they come from?

- What employee educational programs do you have in place to promote health literacy? What patient educational programs do you have in place to promote health literacy?

- Do you have a team in place dedicated to ensuring that all patient-facing documents and materials have been reviewed for health literacy needs?

CHAPTER SEVEN

WHAT ARE THE NEXT STEPS ON YOUR JOURNEY TOWARD HEALTH EQUITY?

- Share a story from within your organization when a failure to provide communication in a patient's preferred language held important repercussions for the patient's health outcome.

- Have you conducted a survey to establish benchmarks to gauge patient perspectives on the effectiveness of your language access services? Do you have data that reveals what languages are spoken by the patients you serve and for the dominant languages present in your service area?

- What is your current approach to language translation services? Do you have data to suggest your current approach is effective or sufficient?

- Do you have system-wide protocols in place for making certain all written materials produced are held to health literacy standards? Do you have uniform requirements for all written materials to be examined for cultural competence? Are all documents that are patient facing available in multiple languages? Is language interpretation available for written documents for patients whose preferred language is something other than those that are dominant in your service area?

- Have you developed a mechanism for making certain that patients who need translation services have those services provided throughout the continuum of their care?

CHAPTER EIGHT

WHAT ARE THE NEXT STEPS ON YOUR JOURNEY TOWARD HEALTH EQUITY?

- Share a story from within your organization for when a spontaneous or happenchance community encounter led to the creation of a formal partnership.

- Share a story from your organization where an essential truth about the relationship between place, community, and health was revealed to you.

- Can you identify communities in your area that are severely underserved or that have poor healthcare access? What leaders and what organizations do you have connections with whom you might partner?

- Do you have specific partnerships formed with organizations that represent niche and minority community members in the area you serve?

- Do your service area demographics support particular faith-based communities that have leverage in their followers' lives?

CHAPTER NINE

WHAT ARE THE NEXT STEPS ON YOUR JOURNEY TOWARD HEALTH EQUITY?

- Share a story from within your organization in which one of your diverse suppliers has had a ripple effect for improving community economic development.

- What percentage of your total supplier spend comes from minority business enterprises, women-, veteran-, disabled-, or LGTBQIA+ owned businesses?

- What peer-to-peer mechanisms do you have in place for informal mentoring, discussion, and coordination specific to your suppliers?

- Do you have councils, committees, or BERGs that work directly with suppliers to familiarize them on opportunities to work with your organization or to share processes and procedures used by your organization?

- Does your organization have a structured mechanism for encouraging and/or financing innovative development of products and services by suppliers and/or employees?

CHAPTER TEN

WHAT ARE THE NEXT STEPS ON YOUR JOURNEY TOWARD HEALTH EQUITY?

- Do you know how your organization is perceived in the communities you serve? Do you have mechanisms in place for gauging such perceptions?

- Does your organization have the equivalents to our BERGs? If so, do they reflect the specific interests of your patient populations?

- Does your organization have the equivalents to our leadership councils that maintain a specific focus on diversity and inclusion?

- What mechanisms do you have in place for recruiting and retaining a workforce that reflects the communities you serve? What measures has your organization taken to ensure that it recruits the best possible talent?

- What measures do you have in place for sharing the successes and accomplishments of your employees with the larger community?

- Which of the strategies we have outlined for fostering an inclusive workforce do you already have in place?

WHAT ARE THE NEXT STEPS ON YOUR JOURNEY TOWARD HEALTH EQUITY?

- Use the power of storytelling, and share a story from within your organization where the presence of unconscious bias altered a patient outcome.

- Share a story from within your organization where the recognition of the presence of unconscious bias offered an opening for a new and different conversation that fosters a more inclusive culture.

- What education programs do you already have in place to help foster an inclusive environment and to train your team members to face their own unconscious biases?

- How do you measure the effectiveness of your educational outreach on inclusion?

- Do you have a methodology in place for your patients to share their experiences, positive and negative, on whether they were made to feel heard and respected during encounters with your organization?

WHAT ARE THE NEXT STEPS ON YOUR JOURNEY TOWARD HEALTH EQUITY?

- The informal can matter as much as the formal. Have you established reinforcing practices that allow your employees to come to know one another by more than names or titles or roles?

- Do you include patient stories in all presentations?

- What are organizations within your service area that help educate the healthcare workers of tomorrow? Have you formed alliances with them or with the institutions that partner with them?

- What are organizations within your service area that advocate for or provide services to those that represent marginalized groups? Have you formed alliances with them or with the institutions that partner with them?

- Has your healthcare system developed formal guidelines that provide your workforce with mechanisms for how those in positions of authority can champion others?

- Has your healthcare system developed educational materials that can assist employees in learning about allyship and ways that they can support their colleagues?

ENDNOTES

1 Richard Horton. "Offline: COVID-19 is not a pandemic." *The Lancet.* Volume 396, Issue 10255. September 26, 2020: 874. https://www. thelancet.com/pdfs/journals/lancet/PIIS0140-6736(20)32000-6.pdf.

2 Merrill Singerr, Nicola Bulled, Bayla Ostrach, Emily Mendenhall. "Syndemics and the biosocial conception of health." *Syndemics.* Volume 389, Issue 10072. March 4, 2017: 941–950 (accessed via *The Lancet*). https://www.thelancet.com/journals/lancet/article/PIIS0140-6736(17)30640-2/fulltext.

3 Richard Horton. "Offline: COVID-19 is not a pandemic." *The Lancet.* Volume 396, Issue 10255. September 26, 2020: 874. https://www. thelancet.com/journals/lancet/article/PIIS0140-6736(20)32000-6/fulltext.

4 David R. Williams and Michelle Sternthal. "Understanding Racial-ethnic Disparities in Health: Sociological Contributions." *Journal of Health and Social Behavior.* October 8, 2010. https://journals.sagepub.com/doi/10.1177/0022146510383838?url_ver=Z39.88-2003&rfr_id=ori:rid:crossref.org&rfr_dat=cr_pub%3dpubmed.

5 Nambi Ndugga, Latoya Hill, Samantha Artiga, and Noah Parker. "Latest Data on COVID-19 Vaccinations by Race/Ethnicity." Kaiser

Family Foundation. https://www.kff.org/coronavirus-covid-19/issue-brief/latest-data-on-covid-19-vaccinations-race-ethnicity/.

6 "Health equity." Institute for Healthcare Improvement. http://www.ihi.org/Topics/Health-Equity/Pages/default.aspx#:~:text=Health%20equity%20is%20realized%20when,particularly%20problematic%20for%20quality%20improvers.

7 "Social determinants of health." Health People.gov. Office of Disease Prevention and Health Promotion. https://www.healthypeople.gov/2020/topics-objectives/topic/social-determinants-of-health.

8 Reid Wilson. "CDC: Blacks, Hispanics dying of COVID-19 at disproportionately high rates." *The Hill.* October 16, 2020. https://thehill.com/policy/healthcare/521404-blacks-hispanics-dying-of-covid-19-at-disproportionately-high-rates.

9 Sophia Carrlatala and Connor Maxwell. "Health disparities by race and ethnicity." Center for American Progress. May 7, 2020. https://www.americanprogress.org/issues/race/reports/2020/05/07/484742/health-disparities-race-ethnicity/.

10 Heather Burris, James Collins Jr., and Robert Wright. "Racial/ethnic disparities in preterm birth: clues for environmental exposures." *Current Opinion in Pediatrics:* April 2011 - Volume 23 - Issue 2 - p 227-232. https://journals.lww.com/co-pediatrics/Abstract/2011/04000/Racial_ethnic_disparities_in_preterm_birth__clues.17.aspx.

11 Hannah Recht and Lauren Weber. "Black Americans are getting vaccinated at lower rates than white Americans." *Kaiser Health News.* January 17, 2021. https://khn.org/news/article/black-americans-are-getting-vaccinated-at-lower-rates-than-white-americans/.

12 National Center for Health Statistics. "Health, United States, 2011." Centers for Disease Control and Prevention. www.cdc.gov/nchs/hus/contents2011.htm.

13 E. Arias, Vera B. Tejada, and F. Ahmad. "Provisional life expectancy estimates for January through June, 2020."

Vital Statistics Rapid Release; no 10. Hyattsville, MD: National Center for Health Statistics. February 2021. DOI: https://dx.doi.org/10.15620/cdc:100392.

14 Ibid.

15 S. Magnan. "Social determinants of health 101 for health care: five plus five." National Academy of Medicine. October 9, 2017. https://nam.edu/social-determinants-of-health-101-for-health-care-five-plus-five/.

16 Ibid.

17 Social determinants of health: know what affects health. Center for Disease Control and Prevention. https://www.cdc.gov/socialdeterminants/index.htm#:~:text=These%20conditions%20are%20known%20as%20social%20determinants%20of%20health%20(SDOH).&text=Social%20determinants%20of%20health%20(SDOH)%20are%20conditions%20in%20the%20places,of%20life%2Drisks%20and%20outcomes.

18 "Is America's approach to health broken? We have a plan to make America healthier." Association of American Medical Colleges. https://strategicplan.aamc.org/AAMC-StrategicPlan-2020.pdf.

19 R. Hardeman, E. Medina, and R. Boyd. "Stolen breaths." *The New England Journal of Medicine.* July 16, 2020. https://www.nejm.org/doi/full/10.1056/NEJMp2021072.

20 George E. Thibault. "Humanism in medicine: What does it mean and why is it more important than ever?" *Academic Medicine*, Volume 94, Issue 8. August 2019: 1074–1077.

21 "Humanistic physicians—How do they stay that way?" News Blog. Penn Medicine News. August 14, 2014. https://www.pennmedicine.org/news/news-blog/2014/august/humanistic-physicians-how-do.

22 Ibid.

23 "Diversity in medicine: facts and figures 2019." American Association of Medical Colleges. https://www.aamc.org/data-reports/workforce/interactive-data/figure-18-percentage-all-active-physicians-race/ethnicity-2018.

24 "Population distribution by race/ethnicity." State Health Facts. Kaiser Family Foundation. https://www.kff.org/other/state-indicator/distribution-by-raceethnicity/?currentTimeframe=0&sortModel=%7B%22colId%22:%22Location%22,%22sort%22:%22asc%22%7D.

25 Dhruv Khullar. "Even as the U.S. grows more diverse, the medical profession is slow to follow." *The Washington Post.* September 23, 2018. https://www.washingtonpost.com/national/health-science/even-as-the-us-grows-more-diverse-the-medical-profession-is-slow-to-

follow/2018/09/21/6e048d66-aba4-11e8-a8d7-0f63ab8b1370_story.html.

26 Carol M. Chou. "What are the habits of highly humanistic physicians?" Gold Foundation Newsroom. July 31, 2014. https://www.gold-foundation.org/what-are-the-habits-of-highly-humanistic-physicians/.

27 *The Health Gap: The Challenge of an Unequal World.* Bloomsbury Press. London. 2015.

28 Donald Berwick. "The moral determinants of health." *Journal of the American Medical Association.* July 21, 2020, Volume 324, Issue 3.

29 *The Health Gap: The Challenge of an Unequal World.* Bloomsbury Press. London. 2015.

30 Rachel R. Hardeman, Eduardo M. Medina, and Rhea W. Boyd. "Stolen Breaths." *The New England Journal of Medicine.* July 16, 2020. Page 2.

31 Donald Berwick. "The moral determinants of health." *Journal of the American Medical Association.* July 21, 2020 Volume 324, Number 3.

32 Ibid.

33 Ibid.

34 "National prevention strategy." National Prevention Council. US Department of Health and Human Services, Office of the Surgeon General, Washington, DC: 2011. https://www.hhs.gov/sites/default/files/disease-prevention-wellness-report.pdf.

35 Jeffrey L. Rodengen. "Shaping the future of healthcare." Northwell Health. 2016. https://www.northwell.edu/sites/northwell.edu/files/d7/ShapingTheFutureOfHealthcare.pdf.

36 "How to train the doctors of the future: an interview with Lawrence Smith of Hofstra North Shore-LIJ School of Medicine." Rx: The Quiet Revolution. https://rxfilm.org/solutions/how-to-train-the-doctors-of-the-future-interview-lawrence-smith-lij-hofstra-university-school-of-medicine/.

37 Joseph R. Betancourt, Sarah Beiter, and Alden Landry. "Improving quality, achieving equity, and increasing diversity in healthcare." *Journal of Best Practices in Health Professions Diversity.* Volume 6, Issue 1. Spring 2013. https://www.jstor.org/stable/26554192.

38 Matthew Weinstock. "An action plan to improve equity, quality." Hospitals and Health Networks. May 1, 2011. https://www.hhnmag.com/

articles/4284-an-action-plan-to-improve-equity-quality.

39 *Evidence-Based Medicine and the Changing Nature of Healthcare: 2007 IOM Annual Meeting Summary.* Institute of Medicine (US). Washington, DC: National Academies Press (US). 2008. https://www.ncbi.nlm.nih.gov/books/NBK52825/.

40 Institute of Medicine (US) Committee on Health and Behavior: Research, Practice, and Policy. Health and Behavior: The Interplay of Biological, Behavioral, and Societal Influences. Washington (DC): National Academies Press (US). 200. https://www.ncbi.nlm.nih.gov/books/NBK43732/.

41 IFDHE AHA Institute for Diversity and Health Equity. https://ifdhe.aha.org/2020-02-04-ifdhe-equity-care-pledge-form.

42 "Nondiscrimination in health and health education programs or activities, delegation of authority." A Rule by the Centers for Medicare & Medicaid Services. Section 92.101. https://ecfr.federalregister.gov/current/title-45/subtitle-A/subchapter-A/part-92/subpart-B/section-92.101.

43 "Health literacy: report of the Council on Scientific Affairs." Ad Hoc Committee on Health Literacy for the Council on Scientific Affairs, American Medical Association. *JAMA*. Volume 218, Issue 6. February 10, 1999: 552–7.

44 Marie T. Brown and Christine A. Sinsky. "Medication adherence: we didn't ask and they didn't tell." *Family Practice Management.* Volume 20, Issue 2. March–April 2013: 25–30. https://www.aafp.org/fpm/2013/0300/p25.html.

45 "Race, ethnicity, and language data: standardization for health care quality improvement." Agency for Healthcare Research and Quality. https://www.ahrq.gov/research/findings/final-reports/iomracereport/reldata5.html.

46 Leah S. Karliner, Elizabeth A. Jacobs, Alice Hm Chen, and Sunita Mutha. "Do professional interpreters improve clinical care for patients with limited English proficiency? a systematic review of the literature." *Health Services Research.* Volume 42, Issue 2. April 2007: 727–54. https://www.ncbi.nlm.nih.gov/pmc/articles/PMC1955368/.

47 Leah S. Karliner. "When patients and providers speak different languages." Patient Safety Network. Agency for Healthcare Research and Quality. April 1, 2018. https://psnet.ahrq.gov/web-mm/

when-patients-and-providers-speak-different-languages.

48 Northwell Health. "Reigniting humanism in healthcare: unlocking the power of diversity through community partnerships." 10th Annual Diversity, Inclusion and Health Equity Summit. https://onlinexperiences. com/scripts/Server.nxp?LASCmd=L:0&AI=1&ShowKey=108565&LoginT ype=0&InitialDisplay=1&ClientBrowser=0&DisplayItem=NULL&LangL ocaleID=0&SSO=1&RFR=NULL.

49 Kate Rope. "Thanks to COVID-19, we can no longer sweep health-care disparities under the rug: Why your ZIP code matters more than your genetic code." The Well by Northwell. April 10, 2020. https://thewell. northwell.edu/deep-dive/geography-health-inequality.

50 Andy Posner. "The problem with the parable about teaching a man to fish." Andy Posner.org. July 28, 2018. https://www.andyposner. org/2018/07/28/problem-parable-teaching-man-woman-fish/.

51 Alexis Bateman, Ashley Barrington, and Katie Date. "Why you need a supplier diversity program." *Harvard Business Review.* April 17, 2020. https://hbr.org/2020/08/why-you-need-a-supplier-diversity-program.

52 Judith Warner, Nora Ellmann, and Diana Boesch. "The women's leadership gap." Center for American Progress. November 20, 2018. https:// www.americanprogress.org/issues/women/reports/2018/11/20/461273/ womens-leadership-gap-2/.

53 Emma Hinchlife. "The female CEOs on this year's Fortune 500 just broke three all-time records." *Fortune.* June 2, 2021. https:// fortune.com/2021/06/02/female-ceos-fortune-500-2021-women-ceo-list-roz-brewer-walgreens-karen-lynch-cvs-thasunda-brown-duckett-tiaa/?utm_source=email&utm_medium=newsletter&utm_ campaign=broadsheet&utm_content=2021060213pm&tpcc=n lbroadsheet.

54 Shelby Livingston. "Fostering diversity for the next generation of healthcare leaders." *Modern Healthcare.* October 13, 2018. https:// www.modernhealthcare.com/article/20181013/NEWS/181019970/ fostering-diversity-for-the-next-generation-of-healthcare-leaders.

55 "Diversity in medicine: facts and figures 2019." Association of American Medical Colleges. https://www.aamc.org/data-reports/ workforce/interactive-data/figure-18-percentage-all-active-physicians-race/

ethnicity-2018.

56 "Sex, race, and ethnic diversity of U.S. health occupations (2011–2015)." Health Resources and Services Administration. US Department of Health and Human Services. August 2017. https://bhw.hrsa.gov/sites/default/files/bureau-health-workforce/data-research/diversity-us-health-occupations.pdf.

57 Health Professionals for Diversity Coalition. "Fact sheet: the need for diversity in the health care workforce." https://www.aapcho.org/wp/wp-content/uploads/2012/11/NeedForDiversityHealthCareWorkforce.pdf.

58 Ibid.

59 Marsala Alsan, Owen Garrick, and Grant Graziani. "Does diversity matter for health? Experimental evidence from Oakland." NBER Working Paper No. 24787. August 2019. https://www.nber.org/system/files/working_papers/w24787/w24787.pdf.

60 Ibid.

61 Vivian Hunt, Dennis Layton, and Sara Prince. "New research makes it increasingly clear that companies with more diverse workforces perform better financially." McKinsey & Company. January 1, 2015. https://www.mckinsey.com/business-functions/organization/our-insights/why-diversity-matters#

62 "Diversity at medical schools makes stronger doctors, study shows." *Science Daily.* September 10, 2008. https://www.sciencedaily.com/releases/2008/09/080909205615.htm.

63 Verna Myers. The Verna Myers Company. https://www.vernamyers.com/.

64 "Heart attacks in women more likely to be missed." University of Leeds. August 30, 2016. https://www.leeds.ac.uk/news/article/3905/heart_attacks_in_women_more_likely_to_be_missed.

65 Kelly Hoffman, Sophie Trawalter, Jordan Axt, and M. Norman Oliver. "Racial bias in pain assessment and treatment recommendations, and false beliefs about biological differences between blacks and whites." Proceedings of the National Academy of Sciences. April 19, 2016. https://www.ncbi.nlm.nih.gov/pmc/articles/PMC4843483/.

66 Ilaria Schlitz. "The bias inside: a conversation with psychologist Jennifer Eberhardt." Behavioral Scientist. May 29, 2019. https://behavioralscientist.

org/the-bias-inside-a-conversation-with-psychologist-jennifer-eberhardt/.

67 Ibid.

68 Robert Roswell, Courtney Cogburn, Jack Tocco, et al. "Cultivating empathy through virtual reality: advancing conversations about racism, inequity, and climate in medicine." *Academic Medicine.* Journal of the Association of American Medical College. December 2020. Volume 95, Issue 12. 1882–1886. https://journals.lww.com/academicmedicine/toc/2020/12000.

69 Virtual Human Interaction Lab, Stanford University. "1,000 cut journey." https://vhil.stanford.edu/1000cut/.

70 Robert Roswell, Courtney Cogburn, Jack Tocco, et al. "Cultivating empathy through virtual reality: advancing conversations about racism, inequity, and climate in medicine. Academic Medicine. Journal of the Association of American Medical College. Volume 95, Issue 12. December 2020: 1882–1886.

71 "Call to action: structural racism as a fundamental driver of health disparities: A presidential advisory from the American Heart Association." *Circulation.* Volume 122, Issue 24. November 10, 2020: 454–468. https://www.ahajournals.org/doi/10.1161/CIR.0000000000000936.

72 The Anti-Oppression Network. "Allyship." https://theantioppressionnetwork.com/allyship/.

73 Kathryn Stroppel. "Racism: what is it, how it affects us, and why it's everyone's job to do something about it." Synergies. Oregon State University. October 5, 2020. https://synergies.oregonstate.edu/2020/racism-what-it-is-how-it-affects-us-and-why-its-everyones-job-to-do-something-about-it/.

74 "Closing the gap in a generation: health equity through action on the social determinants of health." Final Report of the Commission on Social Determinants of Health. World Health Organization. 2008: 1.

75 "The impact of structural racism on Black Americans." Catalyst: Workplaces that work for women. September 30, 2020. https://www.catalyst.org/research/structural-racism-black-americans/.

76 A. Y. Stith and A. R. Nelson. Institute of Medicine. *Committee on Understanding and Eliminating Racial and Ethnic Disparities in Health Care, Board on Health Policy, Institute of Medicine.* Washington, DC: National Academy Press; 2002. Unequal Treatment: Confronting Racial and Ethnic Disparities in Health Care.

77 Institute of Medicine 2001. *Crossing the Quality Chasm: A*

New Health System for the 21st Century. Washington, DC: The National Academies Press.

78 Ibid.

79 The Michigan Health & Hospital Association. "Eliminating disparities to advance health equity and improve quality." July 2020. file:///C:/Users/markl/Downloads/health_equity_guide.pdf.

80 National Prevention Council, National Prevention Strategy, Washington, DC: US Department of Health and Human Services, Office of the Surgeon General, 2011.

81 Institute of Medicine 2001. *Crossing the Quality Chasm: A New Health System for the 21st Century.* Washington, DC: The National Academies Press. https://doi.org/10.17226/10027.

82 Ani Turner. "The business vase for racial equity, strategy for growth." W. K. Kellogg Foundation and Altarum. April 2018. https://altarum.org/publications/the-business-case-for-racial-equity-a-strategy-for-growth.

83 The Michigan Health & Hospital Association. "Eliminating disparities to advance health equity and improve quality." July 2020. https://www.mha.org/HealthDisparities#:~:text=The%20MHA%20Keystone%20Center%20developed,levels%2C%20and%20resources%20to%20support.

84 R. Wyatt, M. Laderman, L. Botwinick, K. Mate, and J. Whittington. "Achieving health equity: a guide for health care organizations." IHI White Paper. Cambridge, Massachusetts: Institute for Healthcare Improvement; 2016. http://www.ihi.org/resources/Pages/IHIWhitePapers/Achieving-Health-Equity.aspx.

85 George E. Thibault. "Humanism in medicine: what does it mean and why is it more important than ever?" *Academic Medicine*, Volume 94, Issue 8. August 2019: 1074–1077.

86 Ibid.

Printed in the USA
CPSIA information can be obtained
at www.ICGtesting.com
LVHW091511080824
787695LV00001B/48